The Prayers
of
St. Teresa of Avila

The Prayers
of
St. Teresa of Avila

compiled by Thomas Alvarez O.C.D.

New City Press

Published in the United States by New City Press
206 Skillman Avenue, Brooklyn, New York 11211
©1990 New City Press, New York

Introduction, editorial comments, and prayers from the original
manuscript "El Escorial" ("E" in references) translated by Jerry
Hearne from the original Spanish edition
Así oraba Teresa (compiled by Thomas Alvarez)
©1982 Imprenta Monte Carmelo, Burgos, Spain

The prayers of St. Teresa contained in this volume are from *The
Collected Works of St. Teresa of Avila,* Volume I, II and III
©1976, 1980, 1985 ICS Publications, Washington, DC

Cover design by Nick Cianfarani

Library of Congress Cataloging-in-Publication Data:

Teresa, of Avila, Saint, 1515-1582.
    [Así oraba Teresa. English]
    The Prayers of St. Teresa of Avila / [compiled by] Thomas Alvarez
; [introduction and editorial comments translated by Jerry Hearne].
      p. cm.
    Translation of: Así oraba Teresa.
    ISBN 0-911782-76-1 : $8.95
    1. Prayers-- Early works to 1800.   I. Alvarez, Thomas, OCD.
  II. Title. III. Title: The Prayers of St. Teresa of Avila.
BX2179.T3A7513 1990
242'.802 – dc20

                                                          89-48237

Printed in the United States of America

TABLE OF CONTENTS

INTRODUCTION

A Note To The Reader

This book is a collection of the personal prayers of Saint Teresa of Jesus. They have been selected from her writings, except for her very last prayer, which she pronounced aloud before dying to Alba de Tormes, and which was also overheard by a nurse, Sister Anna of Saint Bartholomew.

Before you begin your reading, we would like to provide you with some useful background and suggestions.

I — *Teresa of Jesus is a teacher of prayer.* There are not many who can teach the language of "speaking with God," but Teresa is one of them. If you want to attend her school, however, it is not enough to hear her speak about prayer. You must observe her pray.

As far back as her youth, Teresa's unsettled spirit was of no little disturbance to her. Her thirst for God could not be satisfied by books or theories. Furthermore, she was unable to find a teacher who could speak to her of the experience of God. For her, this lack of experience only added up to many useless words and a considerable delay along the journey! Finally, when she arrived at "knowing through experience," how surprised she was to see that her own words became contagious, and that they incited enthusiasm in others. This held true especially for a Dominican professor and friend, Pedro Ibanez, who began to embark on an experience of God similar to hers. The same happened for the novices who lived with her at the convent of Saint Joseph in Avila and for her friends in secular society. Further still, for her brother, Lawrence, who had just returned from America.

At this stage of her life, Teresa no longer sets any resistance against the interior impulse of the spirit, nor does she yield to any temptation to false modesty. She speaks and writes in total freedom so that beginners in prayer would not be deprived of a teacher. She does not want anyone to lose heart due to inexperience.

II — With the help of her *cell* and her *books,* Teresa of Jesus becomes a teacher of prayer. This humble and narrow cell of hers, sealed within the walls of the convent of Saint Joseph in Avila, served the dual function of school and sanctuary. It became the classroom and desk where she could speak intimately with God. It was a place for contemplation. Here she teaches the way of prayer to Sister Anna, to Teresita, and to many others. Here she experiences the frequent raptures that involve her intimate encounter with her Lord.

Her writings, too, become both school and sanctuary. They serve as lessons, but above all as a workshop. Choose at random any one of her works. It may happen that the page you uncover speaks more about roads and journeys than about prayer. What you can be certain of, however, is that she will introduce you to the presence of the Other. Teresa, the writer, will give you details of a typical event she can hardly avoid mentioning: her encounter and dialogue with God. The underlying secret to her teaching method appears to be "never write about prayer without placing yourself in an attitude of prayer before the reader."

III — *The two tempos of the Teresian teaching method.* In teaching "prayer," Teresa has a story to tell. She too, as a child, began to experience an awareness of God. Then she got side-tracked and refrained from prayer for a period of time, only to take it up again. She struggled. She made her way about in a zig zag that finally pointed to her journey's principal direction. Prayer is a journey that meets obstacles to overcome along the way. The journey demands commitment, the practice of evangelical virtues, a "determined determination."

As in the seeding and irrigation of a field of crops, the dynamics of growth and cultivation come into play. The way of prayer can also be compared to climbing the inside of a castle. Teresa herself will say that prayer calls for more than words or thoughts directed to God. It is friendship. God is a friend. Prayer is "developing a friendship with the person who we know loves us."

All the same, the true guide to experience does not consist in telling the reader the story of one's own journey, and not even in communicating personal convictions. Teresa chooses to place herself in prayer before God, and with him. She knows that there are secret channels of communication that lie within all of us into which we pass along to one another our emotions, our feeling for poetry and for beauty . . . and also our sense of God. Teresa, because she lives in the presence of God, communicates precisely this. One might say that it is easy for her to dialogue with him. She engages in conversation with him in complete truth, void of unnecessary formalities. She cannot help but have an effect on those who pass near her, or who listen to her words.

Thus, an endless production of "prayers" flow from her pen. They appear unexpectedly in the midst of a narrative account, while still maintaining dialogue with the reader.

This is her characteristic trait as a writer. She reaches two different planes by addressing two different readers: the common reader as ourselves, and the Other reader, her Lord and "her Majesty." She shifts from one to the Other, suddenly changing style. To speak to the Second in the presence of the first, we can say, is the most effective way of teaching how to develop a relationship with a great Friend. This is the wellspring of her numerous prayers and of the wealth they contain. They are like precious jewels; rays of light. This is the reason for their careful selection and sequence.

IV — *How the selection was organized.* This collection is not simply a random gathering of pearls. The order in which the works of Saint Teresa appear (*The Book of Her Life, The Way of Perfection, Meditations On the Song of Songs,* abbreviated *Life, Way, Meditations...*) follow a teaching method. You will notice the varying tones and expressions in her writings: the soliloquies inserted into the narrative of *The Book of Her Life,* the pauses for prayer with the reader that interrupt her lesson in *The Way of Perfection,* the forcible *Soliloquies* composed in the form of psalms.

— In *The Book of Her Life,* Teresa, while narrating the events of her life-story, relives them at the same time. Not only does she recount these episodes to her readers, but as we mentioned before, she addresses herself to God. Thus, the first series of prayers appear in the form of soliloquies, as in Saint Augustine's *Confessions,* which Teresa had recently read.

— In *The Way of Perfection,* Teresa weaves together a lesson in prayer and a conversation with God. She reaches two different planes, one horizontal, the other vertical. It's as if it were impossible for her to speak of the Church, the Eucharist, living water, love . . . without turning her thoughts to God. Shifting from one plane to the other, she knows fully well that the prayers she introduces into her lessons can be both formative and elevating. For her this is the best way to help the reader grasp what she is trying to say.

— Next are the two books *Meditations On the Song of Songs* and *The Book of Her Foundations.* In one, Teresa raises her heart to God by way of the verses of the Song of Songs, and in the other by contemplating the changing events of her wandering lifestyle. In short, through the word of God in the Bible and through the word of God present in life itself.

— Teresa also wrote a book in which she allowed herself the luxury of writing in pure soliloquy, directed solely to him, to praise him, to question him, to petition him, or to make an offering to him as though she were a priestess of prayer. They are her *Soliloquies:* seventeen prayers written from the depth of contemplation. It is Teresa's book of psalms. To better appreciate them, we suggest that you read them slowly. We tried to aid the reader by writing an introduction to each one so as to set their tone.

— And finally, we present her *poetry.* The stanzas you will read reveal two principal aspects of her prayer. One, a sense of beauty and lyrical expression, which accompany her prayer life and contemplation. The second is a communication of joy, both personal and that of a group, which in Teresa possesses both human warmth and a religious dimension. These verses were also intended for praising God as a people gathered together in prayer (the Carmelite community).

— To round out our selection we have also added a bouquet of prayers that begin with the words "May He be blessed." They are personal hymns of Teresa's that vividly reflect her unbridled way of giving praise to God in the midst of telling her life story, or recalling or reliving moments of her past, or when she is frightened about something. They are her own versions of the psalmic praises in the Bible.

— Teresa's works are not exhausted here. We have had to leave out an entire group which can be found in her *Letters* and *Correspondence*.

Remember that the objective of this book is a very practical one. It is to introduce you to Teresa's school of prayer. To bring you close to her as she prays. To abandon you to the effects of her words. To surround you with her sense of God and humanity. To invite you to pray in communion with her.

This is the same manner in which we would pray along with the biblical psalmists, or even with Jesus himself, the Teacher, when we recite the words, "Our Father, who art in heaven."

Thomas Alvarez, OCD

PRAYERS FROM *THE BOOK OF HER LIFE*

The first book written by Teresa, The Book of Her Life, *was an autobiography, which for her served more than a mere recounting of her past. It became an opportunity to relive it as well. While she writes, she also wants to gain back her past, redeem and restore it to health, and fill it with love and religious meaning.*

In her writing she creates space for a religious dimension inhabited by three persons: Teresa, God, and the reader.

Teresa, by now over fifty years old, returns to her past in order to give it back to God, and to tell its story to the reader.

God, as in the biblical narratives, is always present and plays the main role in the intimate, personal drama of the author.

The readers are a group of beginner disciples, Teresa's close friends. They are just a few — three or four. Fascinated by her account of the work of grace, they are desirous to penetrate the unique experience of God that absorbs her soul.

Out of this context where we find the three characters of her story, Teresa's words emerge. When she addresses the reader, they take on the form of narrative accounts and introspective reflections. When she addresses herself to God, her words become prayer in a way similar to the soliloquies of Saint Augustine in his Confessions.

Whatever situation brought to life from her past, whether concerning her family, her childhood, moments of bitterness, struggle, sin, progress, grace . . . all become a reason and pretext for prayer, love, gratitude, supplication, and praise. It's as though Teresa were committed to reversing the course of streaming waters in order to channel them back to their source. Her whole past becomes motivation for prayer, all the way up to the present moment as she writes the pages of her notebook.

Teresa is fully aware that her words carry her to God "in the presence of the reader." Moreover, she writes with the secret intention to provoke and draw the reader into the dynamism of her luminous ascent.

Thus her prayers can become our own.

1.
FACING THE MYSTERY OF HER OWN LIFE

Teresa of Jesus writes The Book of Her Life. *At the age of fifty she begins her autobiography by recalling her family and childhood: the newness of life, the love of her parents and brothers and sisters, the first books she read, her escape from home in search of martyrdom, games, her mother's death . . . In front of the mystery of circumstances of both light and darkness that repeatedly follow one another, she interrupts her story and turns to God:*

O my Lord, since it seems You have determined to save me, I beseech Your Majesty that it may be so. And since You have granted me as many favors as You have, don't You think it would be good (not for my gain but for Your honor) if the inn where You have so continually to dwell were not to get so dirty?

(Life, 1:8)

2.
THE GOD OF MY YOUTH

Teresa recalls her youth. The decisive moment of her religious calling. The struggle to follow its call. Her novitiate and profession between the ages of twenty and twenty-two. The zeal and self-denial that exhausts her health. In poor health and now outside of the monastery, she advances on the way of personal prayer. At first she experiences progress, and then none whatsoever. Later, she will experience the humiliation of her failure. Amidst this entanglement of memories, a prayer of gratitude to God springs from her heart:

I often marvelled to think of the great goodness of God, and my soul delighted in seeing His amazing magnificence and mercy. May He be blessed by all, for I have seen clearly that He does not fail to repay, even in this life, every good desire. As miserable and imperfect as my deeds were, this Lord of mine improved and perfected them and gave them value, and the evils and sins He then hid. His Majesty even permitted that the eyes of those who saw these sins be blinded, and He removed these sins from their memory. He gilds my faults; the Lord makes a virtue shine that He himself places in me—almost forcing me to have it.

May He be forever blessed who put up with me for so long. Amen.

(Life, 4:10-11)

3.
FIDELITY

Teresa calls to mind a friendship during her youth, and how she lived it in such faithfulness and disinterest in self. Her faithfulness to her God-friend had not been as crystal clear. She tells him so:

Oh blindness of the world! You would have been served, Lord, if I had been most ungrateful to all that world and not the least bit ungrateful to You! But it has been just the reverse because of my sins.

May He be blessed forever. May it please His Majesty that I die rather than ever cease to love Him.

(Life, 5:4-11)

4.
MAY YOU BE BLESSED

At the age of twenty-four Teresa is struck by a very serious illness, grave enough to place her in a coma for four days. She is left paralyzed for the next eight months. During this time her faithfulness to God weakens, undoubtedly due also to the effects of her illness. Now at the age of fifty, she sees that he did not abandon her. She blesses and acknowledges him for this and confesses:

May You be blessed forever! Although I abandoned You, You did not abandon me so completely as not to turn to raise me up by always holding out Your hand to me. And oftentimes, Lord, I did not want it; nor did I desire to understand how often You called me again, as I shall now tell.

(Life, 6:9)

5.
O GREATNESS OF GOD

Teresa is a religious for several years now. Though her health has turned for the better, her spirit has grown lukewarm. She yields to temptations to engage in friendships on a mere human level and spends her free time in aimless conversation. Two mysterious warnings accost her: the countenance of Christ and the incident with the toad. Nevertheless, they only amount to momentary tremors. In her narrative she turns to God . . . grateful and penitent.

As the sins increased I began to lose joy in virtuous things and my taste for them. I saw very clearly, my Lord, that these were failing me because I was failing You.

Oh, the greatness of God! With how much care and pity You were warning me in every way, and how little it benefited me!

*

O Lord of my soul! How can I extol the favors You gave me during these years! And how at the time when I offended You most, You quickly prepared me with an extraordinary repentance to taste Your favors and gifts! Indeed, my King, You, as One who well knew what to me would be most distressing, chose as a means the most delicate and painful punishment. With wonderful gifts You punished my sins!

*

For in falling I had many friends to help me; but in rising I found myself so alone that I am now amazed I did not remain ever fallen. And I praise the mercy of God, for it was He alone who gave me His hand. May He be blessed forever and ever. Amen.

(Life, 7:1, 8, 19, 22)

6.
OH WHAT A GOOD FRIEND YOU ARE, MY LORD!

Teresa reminds the reader that "prayer is friendship." It is even something more: it is building a friendship "with the One who is already our Friend" (God or Christ).
Teresa knows very well that for two persons to become friends they must be in tune with one another: "their personal conditions must coincide with one another." God—she ponders—is a friend by an entirely different condition. What a commitment on his part to lower himself and make himself accessible to the human-friend condition, even to a person like Teresa! Thus she writes, "realizing the gain I receive in enjoying his friendship and how much he loves me, I can manage to tolerate the effort to stay at length with those who are so different from me."

O infinite goodness of my God, for it seems to me I see that such is the way You are and the way I am! O delight of angels, when I see this I desire to be completely consumed in loving You! How certainly You do suffer the one who suffers to be with You! Oh, what a good friend You make, my Lord! How You proceed by favoring and enduring. You wait for the other to adapt to Your nature, and in the meanwhile You put up with his! You take into account, my Lord, the times when he loves You, and in one instant of repentance You forget his offenses.

I do not know, my Creator, why it is that every one does not strive to reach You through this special friendship, and why those who are wicked, who are not conformed to Your will, do not, in order that You make them good, allow You to be with them at least two hours each day, even though they may not be with You, but with a thousand disturbances from worldly cares and thoughts, as was the case with me. Through this effort they make to remain in such good company (for You see that in the beginning they cannot do more, nor afterward, sometimes), You, Lord, force the devils not to attack them, so that each day the devils' strength against them lessens; and You give them the victory over the devils. Yes, for You do not kill—life of all lives!—any of those who trust in You and desire You for friend. But You sustain the life of the body with more health, and You give life to the soul.

(Life, 8:6)

7.
THE FIRST STEPS IN PRAYER

After her recent conversion, Teresa prayed in this way:

This is the method of prayer I then used: since I could not reflect discursively with the intellect, I strove to picture Christ within me, and it did me greater good—in my opinion—to picture Him in those scenes where I saw Him more alone. It seemed to me that being alone and afflicted, as a person in need, He had to accept me. I had many simple thoughts like these.

The scene of His prayer in the garden, especially, was a comfort to me; I strove to be His companion there. If I could, I thought of the sweat and agony He had undergone in that place. I desired to wipe away the sweat He so painfully experienced, but I recall that I never dared to actually do it, since my sins appeared to me so serious. I remained with Him as long as my thoughts allowed me to, for there were many distractions that tormented me.

(Life, 9:4)

8.
HE TRANSFORMED ME, AS THOUGH FROM A DUNGHEAP
INTO A DELIGHTFUL GARDEN OF FLOWERS

Teresa retraces the turning point of her life: the moment of her conversion.

"Making up one's mind and holding strong" took her years to accomplish. She finally said her yes to Christ. Then everything changed. She felt as though her soul had become a garden of flowers, herbs, and running water. "It gave me great delight to consider my soul as a garden in which the Lord came to walk about" (Life, 14:9).

May His Majesty be blessed for everything and served by me on account of who He is. For my Lord knows well that in writing this I have no other aim than that He be praised and extolled a little when it is seen that in so filthy and malodorous a dungheap He should make a garden with so many delicate flowers. May His Majesty be pleased that through my own fault I do not pull them up again and let the garden return to what it was.

(Life, 10:9)

9.
THE PRAYER OF BEGINNERS

"Whoever sees in himself this determination has no reason, no reason whatsoever to fear. Once you are placed in so high a degree as to desire to commune in solitude with God and abandon the pastimes of the world, the most has been done. Praise His Majesty for that and trust in His goodness who never fails His friends. Let His Majesty lead the way along the path He desires. We belong no longer to ourselves but to Him. He grants us a great favor in wanting us to desire to dig in His garden and be in the presence of its Lord who is certainly present with us. Should He desire that for some these plants and flowers grow by the water they draw, which He gives from this well, and for others without it, what difference does it make to me?" (Life, 11:12).

Do, Lord, what You desire. May I not offend You. Don't let the virtues be lost, if You only out of Your goodness have already given me some. I desire to suffer, Lord, since You suffered. Let Your will be done in me in every way, and may it not please Your Majesty that something as precious as Your love be given to anyone who serves you only for the sake of consolations.

(Life, 11:12)

10.
FOR THEOLOGIANS

Teresa prays for the theologians. She is certain that some of them have caused her to suffer. Still, they are men of light and knowledge, the ones "who are familiar with the Sacred Scriptures" and "find in them the truth of the good spirit" (Life, 13:18).

Her prayer for these men is one of intercession, asking God to bestow them with graces and praising him for the work they do.

May You be blessed, Lord, who have made me so unable and unprofitable! But I praise You very much because You awaken so many to awaken us. Our prayer for those who give us light should be unceasing. In the midst of tempests as fierce as those the Church now endures, what would we be without them? If some have gone bad, the good ones shine more brilliantly. May it please the Lord to keep them in His hands and help them so that they might help us, amen.

(Life, 13:21)

11.
GOD-FRIEND

This prayer takes its inspiration from the biblical passage: "I found my delight in the sons of men" (Prv 8:31). Listening to these words cause Teresa to shed tears of delight and consolation. So amazed is she to the point of "being carried outside of herself."

O my Lord and my God! I cannot say this without tears and great joy of soul! How You desire, Lord, thus to be with us and to be present in the Sacrament (for in all truth this can be believed since it is so, and in the fullness of truth we can make this comparison); and if it were not for our fault, we could rejoice in being with You, and You would be glad to be with us since You say that Your delight is to be with the children of men. O my Lord! What is this? As often as I hear these words, they bring me great consolation; they did so even when I was very far gone. Is it possible, Lord, that there be a soul that reaches the point where You bestow similar favors and gifts, and understands that You are to be with it, that goes back to offending You after so many favors and after such striking demonstrations of the love You have for it which cannot be doubted since the effects of it are obvious? Yes, there certainly is one, and not one who has done this once but done it many times — for it is I. And may it please your goodness, Lord, that I might be the only ungrateful one and the only one who has done such terrible evil and shown such excessive ingratitude. But even from this evil, Your infinite goodness has drawn out something worthwhile; and the greater the evil, the more resplendent the wonder of Your mercies. And how many are the reasons I can sing Your mercies forever!

I beseech You, my God, that it may be so and that I may sing them without end since You have deigned to bestow upon me mercies so outstanding they amaze those who see them; and as for me, they frequently carry me out of myself to praise You the better. By remaining in myself without You, I could do nothing, my Lord, but return to cutting the garden flowers in such a way that this miserable ground would once more serve for a trash heap as it did previously. Do not permit it, Lord, or desire the loss of the soul You bought with so many labors and which You have so often gone back again to rescue and save from the teeth of the terrifying dragon.

(Life, 14:10-11)

12.
ON THE BRINK OF ECSTASY

Teresa is speaking of prayer. She would like to be able to explain to four of her closest disciples a way of prayer that borders on a madness of love that makes one burst into "a thousand holy follies." Whoever finds oneself to be immersed in this kind of prayer "would wish that both body and soul would break into pieces" due to the joy and giving of praise one experiences.
Teresa experienced this kind of madness that very morning in the Eucharist. She relives it now as she is writing. Interrupting her dialogue with her four friends, she turns to God.

May You be blessed forever, Lord! May all things praise You forever! Since while I write this I am not freed from such holy, heavenly madness coming from Your goodness and mercy — for You grant this favor without any merits on my part at all — either desire, my King, I beseech You, that all to whom I speak become mad from Your love, or do not permit that I speak to anyone! Either ordain, Lord, that I no longer pay attention to anything in the world, or take me out of it!

O true Lord and my Glory! How delicate and extremely heavy a cross You have prepared for those who reach this state! "Delicate" because it is pleasing; "heavy" because there come times when there is no capacity to bear it; and yet the soul would never want to be freed from it unless it were for the sake of being with You. When it recalls that it hasn't served You in anything and that by living it can serve You, it would want to carry a much heavier cross and never die until the end of the world. It finds no rest in anything except in doing You some small service. It doesn't know what it wants, but it well understands that it wants nothing other than You.

(Life, 16:4-5)

13.
AWAY FROM INNER CONFUSION

The imagination is the "madperson of the house," who goes into tantrums even while we pray. Teresa, against her will, tries to be tolerant of them. She speaks to God about this and asks him to grant her inner peace and order.

"When, my God, will my soul be completely joined together in Your praise and not broken in pieces, unable to make use of itself?"
(Life, 17:5)

14.
OH HOW GOOD YOU ARE!

In her own life story, Teresa experienced the most fundamental truth of the Bible: God takes interest in the lives of all human persons; he extends himself to them and loves them. Surprisingly, he loves her too. His love is greatness, magnificence, and sovereign gift. Though Teresa experiences this, her mind is unable to grasp it. She needs to tell him so.

O my Lord, how good You are! May You be blessed forever! May all things praise You, my God, for You have so loved us that we can truthfully speak of this communication which You engage in with souls even in our exile! And even in the case of those who are good, this still shows great generosity and magnanimity. In fact, it is Your communication, my Lord; and You give it in the manner of who You are. O infinite Largess, how magnificent are Your works! It frightens one whose intellect is not occupied with things of the earth that he has no intellect by which he can understand divine truths. That you bestow such sovereign favors on souls that have offended You so much certainly brings my intellect to a halt; and when I begin to think about this, I'm unable to continue. Where can the intellect go that would not be a turning back since it doesn't know how to give you thanks for such great favors? Sometimes I find it a remedy to speak absurdities.
(Life, 18:3)

15.
LORD, LOOK WHAT YOU ARE DOING!

Teresa feels that she is the recipient of so many graces on the part of God to the point of being "full of graces," overflowing with them. She asks him whether he forgot that Teresa is a sinful woman. This is

Peter's attitude before Jesus: "Go away from me for I am a sinner."
"It often happens to me that just after I receive these graces, or in
the very moment that God begins to give them to me, I break out into
thoughts of this kind."

Lord, look what You are doing. Don't forget so quickly my great wickedness. Now that in order to pardon me You have forgotten it, I beseech You to remember it that You might put a limit on Your favors. Don't my Creator, pour such precious liqueur in so broken a bottle; You have already seen at other times how I only spill and waste it. Don't place a treasure like this in a place where cupidity for life's consolations is still not cast off as it should be; otherwise it will be badly squandered. How is it that You surrender the strength of this city and the keys to its fortress to so cowardly a mayor who at the enemy's first attack allows him entrance? Don't let Your love be so great, eternal King, as to place in risk such precious jewels. It seems, my Lord, that the occasion is given for esteeming them but little since You put them in the power of a thing so wretched, so lowly, so weak and miserable, and of so little importance. For although she strives with Your help not to lose them (and there is need for more than a little effort because of what I am), she cannot make use of them to win over anyone. In sum, she is a woman; and not a good but a wretched one. It seems that the talents are not only hidden but even buried by being placed in such vile earth. You are not accustomed, Lord, to bestow on a soul grandeurs and favors like these unless for the profit of many. You already know, my God, that with all my heart and will I beseech You and have besought You at times in the past that You grant these favors to someone who would make better use of them for the increase of Your glory—and that I would consider it a blessing to lose the greatest earthly good possessable in order that You do so.

These and other things it often occurred to me to say. I saw afterward my foolishness and lack of humility; the Lord well knows what is fitting and that I would not have the strength in my soul to be saved if His Majesty didn't give it to me through so many favors.

(Life, 18:4-5)

16.
AT THE PEAK OF ECSTASY

The following is a very brief cry of praise, beginning with her
characteristic "May you be blessed." Teresa, just prior to composing
this prayer had written, "My soul, in ecstasy, finding itself before
him—what else ought it do but love him in return? It does not see or

hear anything else save by much effort. There is little it can find satisfaction in. Then, with striking truth, both its past life and the infinite mercy of God reveal themselves in a way that the intellect need not go in search for them, for it beholds there all cooked and prepared what it must consume and contemplate. It perceives that it merits hell, but seeing how it is punished with heavenly delights, it breaks out into hymns of praise to God, just as I long to do in this moment. May you be blessed my Lord!"

May You be blessed, my Lord, that from such filthy mud as I, You make water so clear that it can be served at Your table! May You be praised, O Joy of the angels, for having desired to raise up a worm so vile!

(Life, 19:2)

17.
PRAYER OF THOSE WHO HAVE FALLEN

Even if you fall, pray! God is mercy and greatness. Teresa knows through experience that the strongest temptation of her life is to abandon prayer after having been unfaithful to God. Even "the traitor (the tempter) knows very well that he loses a soul that perseveres in prayer, and for whom all its falls, through the goodness of God, become only helps to take a more energetic leap ahead in his service."

O my Jesus! What a sight it is when You through Your mercy return to offer Your hand and raise up a soul that has fallen in sin after having reached this stage! How such a soul knows the multitude of Your grandeurs and mercies and its own misery! In this state it is in truth consumed and knows Your splendors. Here it doesn't dare raise its eyes, and here it raises them up so as to know what it owes You. Here it becomes a devotee of the Queen of heaven so that she might appease You; here it invokes the help of the saints that fell after having been called by You. Here it seems that everything You give it is undeserved because it sees that it doesn't merit the ground on which it treads. Here, in approaching the sacraments, it has the living faith to see the power that God has placed in them; it praises You because You have left such a medicine and ointment for our wounds and because this medicine not only covers these wounds but also takes them away completely. It is amazed by all this. And who, Lord of my soul, wouldn't be amazed by so much mercy and a favor so large for a betrayal so ugly and abominable? I don't know why my heart doesn't break as I write this! For I am a wretched person!

(Life, 19:5)

18.
THIS GOD WHO NEVER GETS TIRED OF GIVING

A storm of memories. Teresa recalls the many dark years that delayed her journey. She recalls the fear that gripped her the year before as she beheld the mystery of God in the biblical passage, "You are righteous, O Lord, and your judgements are holy." Because of her own experience, she turns to her readers, telling them to "trust in the goodness of God, which is greater than all the evils we can commit."

Souls should remember His words and see what He did with me; before I grew tired of offending Him, His Majesty began to pardon me. He never tires of giving, nor can He exhaust His mercies. Let us not tire of receiving. May He be blessed forever, amen — and may all things praise Him.

(Life, 19:15)

19.
PRAYER OF THE MIGHTY . . . AND OF KINGS

Teresa arrives at "understanding truths." Prayer is a light. She has an impetuous desire to pass it on, to shout out the truth, to cry it out to those who hold authority. Even at the cost of her own life, she would want to tell it to the kings. However, everything keeps her from doing so: her state of monastic, cloistered life, her being a woman, and society itself being what it is. Without renouncing to such a great desire to "cry out," she turns to God to tell it to him.

Blessed is the soul the Lord brings to the understanding of truth!
O Lord! Were You to give me the office by which I could shout this aloud, they would not believe me, as they do not believe many who know how to say this better than I; but at least it would be satisfying to me. It seems to me I would have held my life in little account in order to make known only one of these truths; I don't know what I might have done afterward, for I am not trustworthy. In spite of what I am, I experience great consuming impulses to tell these truths to those who are rulers. When I can do no more, I turn to You, my Lord, to beg of You a remedy for all. And You know well that I would very willingly dispossess myself of the favors You have granted me and give them to the kings, providing I could remain in a state in which I do not offend You; because I know that it would then be impossible for them to consent to the things that are now consented to, nor would these favors fail to bring the greatest blessings.
O my God! Give kings an understanding of their obligations.

(Life, 21:2-3)

20.
JESUS CHRIST CRUCIFIED,
LORD OF MY SOUL AND MY GOOD

Having before her the Humanity of Christ, his evangelical life, his words and sentiments, body and soul, blood and sufferings, passion and death . . . for Teresa God in Jesus is grace, the way, the model, a living book. He is a friend and companion, an ocean of inexhaustible possibilities.
There was a very brief period in Teresa's life where she gave only relative value to all these things in view of her prayer and spiritual life. It was an error she deplored as one of the most dismal distortions of her life. Now she knows that the Humanity of Jesus is "a vast sea of blessings"; that Jesus leaves "nothing undone for those who love Him; in the measure He sees that they receive Him, so He gives and is given. He loves whoever loves Him; how good a beloved! how good a friend! O Lord of my soul! . . ."

O Lord of my soul, who has the words to explain what You give to those who trust in You and to explain what those lose who reach this state and yet remain with themselves! Do not desire a loss like this, Lord, since You do so much in coming to a dwelling place as shabby as mine. May You be blessed forever and ever!

O Lord of my soul and my Good, Jesus Christ crucified! At no time do I recall this opinion I had without feeling pain; it seems to me I became a dreadful traitor — although in ignorance.

Certainly there is no one who can endure thinking all the time about the many trials He suffered. Behold Him here without suffering, full of glory, before ascending into heaven, strengthening some, encouraging others, our companion in the most Blessed Sacrament; it doesn't seem it was in His power to leave us for even a moment. And what a pity it was for me to have left You, my Lord, under the pretext of serving You more! When I was offending You I didn't know You; but how, once knowing You, did I think I could gain more by this path! Oh, what a bad road I was following, Lord! Now it seems to me I was walking on no path until You brought me back, for in seeing You at my side I saw all blessings. There is no trial that it wasn't good for me to suffer once I looked at You as You were, standing before the judges. Whoever lives in the presence of so good a friend and excellent a leader, who went ahead of us to be the first to suffer, can endure all things. The Lord helps us, strengthens us, and never fails; He is a true friend.

(*Life,* 22:17, 3, 6)

21.

OUT OF THE DEPTHS I CRY TO YOU, O LORD

Teresa must submit the mystical graces she receives to the discernment of the theologians. She lives this critical moment in great anxiety as though they were to pass judgment on her soul. Five or six theologians, friends among themselves, convened to express their opinions. "My confessor told me that they all came to the decision that my experience was from the devil, that I shouldn't receive Communion so often, and that I should try to distract myself in such a way that I would not be alone."

*Physically, Teresa suffers from a long-enduring heart ailment that at times keeps her "from daring to remain alone in her room even during the daytime." The theologians took Communion from her and forbid her to be alone, "the only things that gave me comfort, because there was no one person I could confide in since all were against me. When I spoke of the matter, it seemed that some made fun of me as though I were inventing it; others advised my confessor to be careful of me; others said that my experience was clearly from the devil. . . . I received no consolation, neither from heaven nor earth. . . . Gripped by this affliction, I fled from the church and entered an oratory" (*Life, 25:14-17*). Out of the depths of her tribulation, she cries out to the Lord:*

O my Lord, how You are the true friend; and how powerful! When You desire You can love, and You never stop loving those who love You! All things praise You, Lord of the world! Oh, who will cry out for You, to tell everyone how faithful You are to Your friends! All things fail; You, Lord of all, never fail! Little it is, that which You allow the one who loves You to suffer! O my Lord! How delicately and smoothly and delightfully You treat them! Would that no one ever pause to love anyone but You! It seems, Lord, You try with rigor the person who loves You so that in extreme trial he might understand the greatest extreme of Your love. O my God, who has the understanding, the learning, and the new words with which to extol Your works as my soul understands them? All fails me, my Lord; but if You do not abandon me, I will not fail You. Let all learned men rise up against me, let all created things persecute me, let the devils torment me; do not You fail me, Lord, for I already have experience of the gain that comes from the way You rescue the one who trusts in You alone.

(*Life,* 25:17)

22.
THE WORDS OF THE RISEN LORD:
"IT IS I, DO NOT BE AFRAID"

*In the midst of a fierce storm of doubts and persecutions on the part of the theologians (cf. previous prayer) Teresa's form of prayer becomes an intense listening to the evangelical word. "While in this great affliction . . . these words alone were enough to take it away and bring me complete quiet: 'Do not fear, daughter; for I am, and I will not abandon you; do not fear.' It seems to me from the way I felt that many hours would have been necessary and no one would have been able to persuade me to be at peace. And behold by these words alone I was given calm together with fortitude, courage, security, quietude, and light so that in one moment I saw my soul become another. It seems to me that I would have disputed with the entire world that these words came from God. Oh, what a good God!" (*Life, 25:18).*

Oh, how good a Lord and how powerful! He provides not only the counsels but also the remedy! His words are works! Oh, God help me; and how He strengthens faith and increases love!

Hence it is, indeed, that I often recalled the time the Lord commanded the winds to be quiet when the storm arose at sea, and so I said: Who is this that all my faculties obey Him thus, who gives in a moment and in the midst of such great darkness, who softens a heart that seemed like stone, and who gives the water of gentle tears where it seemed there would be dryness for a long time? Who imparts these desires? Who bestows this courage? For it occurred to me to think: What do I fear? What is this? I desire to serve this Lord; I aim for nothing else but to please Him. I want no happiness, no rest, no other good but to do His will (for I felt deeply certain in my opinion that I could make this assertion). If this Lord is powerful, as I see that He is and I know that He is, and if the devils are His slaves (and there is no doubt about this because it's a matter of faith), what evil can they do to me since I am a servant of this Lord and King? Why shouldn't I have the fortitude to engage in combat with all of hell?

(*Life,* 25:18-19)

23.
MY EYES HAVE BEHELD CHRIST

Teresa refers back to an ineffable Christological experience: her first purely spiritual vision of Christ (cf. Life, 27:2). She calls to mind the biblical text from the Song of Songs: "These two lovers gaze directly at each other, as the Bridegroom says to the Bride in the Song of

*Songs" (Life, 27:10). She addresses God as "admirable kindness" and
offers her eyes to him asking faith for "mortals."*

O admirable kindness of God, You allow me to gaze upon You with
eyes that have so badly gazed as have those of my soul. May they,
Lord, become accustomed through this vision not to look at base
things, so that nothing outside of You might satisfy them! O ingratitude of mortals! To what extremes will you go? For I know
through experience that what I say is true and that what can be said
is the least of what You do, Lord, for a soul You bring to such frontiers.
O souls that have begun to practice prayer and have true faith, what
good things can you still seek in this life — leaving aside what is gained
for eternity — that could compare with the least of these favors?

Reflect that it is indeed certain that God gives Himself in this way
to those who give up all for Him. He shows no partiality, He loves
everyone. Nobody has any excuse, no matter how miserable he may
be, since the Lord so acts with me in bringing me to such a state.

(Life, 27:11-12)

24.
A PRAYER OF A WITNESS TO THE RESURRECTION

*Jesus chooses witnesses of his Resurrection. And he appears to them.
First to the disciples. Then to an enemy, Saul, as he travels the road
to Damascus. Finally, to others along the course of Church history.
Among them was Teresa. Like Paul who, while still blinded with light,
tells of his vision in the Acts of the Apostles (26:13), Teresa, stumbling
with words, tells the experience of her own road to Damascus. She
calls to mind that with his mere presence Jesus "makes it known that
he is both man and God, not as he was in the tomb, but as he was
when He came out of the tomb after His Resurrection. Sometimes He
comes with such great majesty that no one could doubt that it is the
Lord Himself. He reveals Himself as so much the Lord of this dwelling
that it seems the soul is completely dissolved; and it sees itself consumed
in Christ." She then shifts from memory to prayer: "O my Jesus!"
(Life, 28:8).*

O my Jesus! Who could make known the majesty with which You
reveal Yourself! And, Lord of all the world and of the heavens, of a
thousand other worlds and of numberless worlds, and of the heavens
that You might create, how the soul understands by the majesty with
which You reveal Yourself that it is nothing for You to be Lord of
the world!

In this vision the powerlessness of all the devils in comparison with
Your power is clearly seen, my Jesus, and it is seen how whoever is

pleasing to You can trample all hell under foot. In this vision the reason is seen why the devils feared when You descended into limbo and why they would have preferred to be in another thousand lower hells in order to flee from such great majesty. I see that You want the soul to know how tremendous this majesty is and the power that this most sacred humanity joined with the Divinity has. In this vision there is a clear representation of what it will be like on Judgment Day to see the majesty of this King and to see its severity toward those who are evil. This vision is the source of the true humility left in the soul when it sees its misery, which it cannot ignore. This vision is the source of confusion and the true repentance for sins; although the soul sees that He shows love, it doesn't know where to hide, and so it is completely consumed.

(Life, 28:8-9)

25.
A PRAYER OF LOVE

Teresa's Christian journey enters into a mysterious region of mystical experience. Her interactions with God have been purified, most essentially her love. Love has become a fire, a wound, the pain of separation, a desire for death, but further still, a desire for a different kind of life. "After a short time His Majesty began as He had promised me to give further indication that it was He by increasing the love of God in me to such a degree that I didn't know where it came from (for it was very supernatural); nor did I procure it. I saw that I was dying with desire to see God, and I didn't know where to seek this life except in death. Some great impulses of this love came upon me in such a way that, even though they were not as unbearable as those I already mentioned before or of such value, I didn't know what to do with myself. For nothing satisfied me, nor could I put up with myself; it truly seemed as if my soul were being wrested from me. O superb contrivance... "(Life, 29:8).

O superb contrivance of my Lord! What delicate skill You use with Your miserable slave! You hide Yourself from me and afflict me with Your love through a death so delightful that the soul would never want to escape from it.*

(Life, 29:8)

---

* This very brief prayer is taken from the chapter in which Teresa recounts the experience of the arrow which inflicts her heart (*Life,* 29). Only if read in this context does it acquire its full significance and effectiveness. The images Teresa employs (fire, wound, arrow, death . . .) are together biblical and experiential. They are

26.
HOW HUMILIATING . . . TO COUNT THE GRAINS OF SAND!

In writing chapters 30 and 31 of her Life, *Teresa makes a disconcerting assessment of her belongings. On one side: she has received a multitude of graces. On the other: she has not practiced a sufficient number of humble services for her fellow Sisters, including acts of humility and acts that concerned the greater good of the community. She states: "I want to mention now the trivial or insignificant actions I performed during the initial phases of my journey . . . the straw that I tried to throw into the fire, for more than that I was unable to do. The Lord accepts everything: may he be blessed forever! By means of these trifles, which are nothing—and a complete nothing I am, since this pained me—little by little one makes progress in deeds. And His Majesty gives value to little things like these that are done for Him, and He gives the help for doing greater things" (Life, 31:23-24). Teresa takes her eyes off her balance sheet and turns to prayer:*

O my Lord! What a shame it is to see so much wickedness and to tell about some grains of sand, which even then I didn't lift from the ground for Your service, since everything I did was enveloped in a thousand miseries! The waters of Your grace didn't flow yet under these grains of sand in order to raise them up. O my Creator! Who could find among so many evils something of substance to relate, since I am telling about the great favors I've received from You! So it is, my Lord, that I don't know how my heart can bear it or how anyone who reads this can fail to abhor me in observing that such marvelous favors were so poorly repaid and that I have no shame, in the end, to recount these services as my own. Yes, I am ashamed, my Lord; but having nothing else to tell about the part I played makes me speak of such lowly beginnings so that anyone who did great things in the beginning may have hope; since it seems the Lord has taken my early actions into account, He will do so more with theirs. May it please His

---

associated especially with the Song of Songs and the Book of Psalms: "How many times when I find myself in this state do I recall the verse of David's: *quemadmodum desiderat cervus ad fontes aquarum;* for I seem to see that it has happened within myself!" (n. 11). Or when explaining the furnace of love. "Here it is not we who lay down the wood, but it seems that the fire has already been kindled and that in an instant someone has thrown us inside. It is not the soul which has caused itself the wound of the Lord's absence, but someone else who at a given moment drives an arrow into the deepest recesses of the heart, leaving it so bewildered that it doesn't know what has inflicted it or what it wants. The soul with such an ailment would always want to be at the point of death" (n. 10). In the Song of Songs it is the man who says, *vulnerasti cor meum.*

Majesty to give me grace so that I might not always remain at the beginning, amen.

(Life, 31:25)

27.
CONCERNING HER MISSION AS A FOUNDRESS

Teresa gives life to her first foundation, the Carmel of Saint Joseph. It was a strong interior impulse that drove her to accomplish this. She was told, "enter in any way you can" into the new house. She threw herself into action. But every detail seemed to unveil a new obstacle. "I went through so many trials of so many kinds that now I'm amazed I was able to suffer them. Sometimes in distress I said: 'My Lord . . .'" (Life, *33:11).*

My Lord, how is it You command things that seem impossible? For if I were at least free, even though I am a woman! But bound on so many sides, without money or the means to raise it or obtain the brief or anything, what can I do, Lord?

(Life, 33:11)

28.
PRAYER FOR A FRIEND

Teresa is at Toledo. She meets up with an old friend at one of the churches in the city. He is a Dominican, a man of high acclaim. Teresa, however, would want him to be more of God than he is. At a certain moment, she turns from writing about her casual friend in order to address her Permanent Friend—from a conversation with a religious to a conversation with God.

He asked me to pray earnestly to God for him, but he had no need to ask since I was already of such a mind that I couldn't have done otherwise. I went to the place where I usually prayed alone and, being deeply recollected, began to talk to the Lord in a foolish way, which I often do without knowing what I'm saying. It is love that is then speaking, and the soul is so transported that I don't notice the difference there is between it and God. Love that knows it possesses His Majesty forgets the soul and thinks it is in Him and, as one without division, speaks absurdities. I recall that after having begged Him with many tears for that soul, that it be truly committed to His service, I said that even though I considered him good this didn't satisfy me, since I wanted him to be very good; and so I said to His Majesty:

"Lord, You must not deny me this favor; see how this individual is fit to be our friend."

O goodness and great humanity of God! You don't look at the words but at the desires and the will with which they are spoken! How do You bear that one like myself should speak so boldly to Your Majesty! May You be blessed forever and ever.

(Life, 34:8-9)

29.
CONCERNING FRIENDSHIP

Teresa is now at the new Carmel of Saint Joseph. Around her is a group of young people who lead the life of Carmel with simplicity and joy. Some of them have left a world behind that consisted of elegant wardrobes, vanities, and a comfortable life. "Here the Lord has given them satisfaction a hundred times over what they have left." In contemplation of this group of generous young people, Teresa gives praise and renders thanks to God.

O my Jesus, what a soul inflamed in Your love accomplishes! How highly we must esteem such a soul and how we must beg the Lord to let it remain in this life! Whoever has this same love must follow after these souls if he can.

(Life, 34:15)

30.
O MY LORD, HOW WELL YOU KNOW HOW
TO DEMONSTRATE YOUR POWER

Teresa is only at the initial stages of her life as a foundress. She has just bought two little houses to establish the first Carmel of Saint Joseph. However, this undertaking demands her absence from Avila and for six months she lives at a mansion of a noblewoman of Toledo. By the height of summer, she must take a step back as she foresees the oncoming of additional painful obstacles. Two biblical passages provide strength for her soul. One she heard from the Lord in the form of a promise: the future Carmel "will be a paradise of delight for Him" (Life, 35:12). The other springs forth from the wellspring of her experience: "you pretend to make the law heavy for us." Power and love become "certainties" of life, a "royal path."

O my Lord, how obvious it is that You are almighty! There's no need to look for reasons for what You want. For, beyond all natural reason, You make things so possible that You manifest clearly there's no need for anything more than truly to love You and truly to leave all for You, so that You, my Lord, may make everything easy.

It fits well here to say that You feign labor in Your law. For I don't see, Lord, nor do I know how the road that leads to You is narrow. I see that it is a royal road, not a path; a road that is safer for anyone who indeed takes it. Very far off are the occasions of sin, those narrow mountain passes and the rocks that make one fall. What I would call a path, a wretched path and a narrow way, is the kind which has on one side, where a soul can fall, a valley far below, and on the other side a precipice: as soon as one becomes careless one is hurled down and broken into pieces.

He who really loves You, my Good, walks safely on a broad and royal road. He is far from the precipice. Hardly has he begun to stumble when You, Lord, give Him Your hand. One fall is not sufficient for a person to be lost, nor are many, if he loves You and not the things of the world. He journeys in the valley of humility. I cannot understand of how wretched is the security that lies in such manifest dangers as following the crowd and how true security lies in striving to make progress on the road of God. Let them turn their eyes to Him and not fear the setting of this Sun of Justice, nor, if we don't first abandon Him, will He allow us to walk at night and go astray.

(Life, 35:13-14)

31.
YOU ARE LORD

For Saint Paul, the encounter with Jesus on the way to Damascus did not prove to be a one-time event. Christ continued to take root in his soul, shaping it with both religious and human sentiments.
Something similar happened to Teresa after her own encounter with Jesus. "A much greater love for and confidence in this Lord began to develop in me when I saw Him as one with whom I could converse so continually. I saw that He was man, even though He was God; that He wasn't surprised by the weaknesses of men; that he understands our miserable make-up, subject to many falls on account of the first sin which he came to repair. I can speak with Him as with a friend, even though He is Lord. I know that He isn't like those we have as lords here on earth, all of whose lordship consists in artificial displays" (Life, *37:5).*

O King of Glory and Lord of all kings! How true that Your kingdom is not armed with trifles, since it has no end! How true that there is no need for intermediaries with You! Upon beholding Your person one sees immediately that You alone, on account of the majesty you reveal, merit to be called Lord. There's no need for people in waiting or for guards in order that one know that You are King. Here on earth, if a king were all by himself, he would fail to be recognized. However much he would want to be recognized as king, he wouldn't be believed; he would have no more to show than anyone else. It's necessary that one see the reason for believing he is a king, and that is the purpose of these artificial displays. If he didn't have them, no one would esteem him at all; the appearance of power doesn't come from him. It is from others that his display of grandeur must come.

O my Lord! O my King! Who now would know how to represent Your majesty! It's impossible not to see that You in Yourself are a great Emperor, for to behold Your majesty is startling; and the more one beholds along with this majesty, Lord, Your humility and the love You show to someone like myself the more startling it becomes. Nevertheless, we can converse and speak with You as we like, once the first fright and fear in beholding Your majesty passes; although the fear of offending You becomes greater. But the fear is not one of punishment, for this punishment is considered nothing in comparison with losing You.

(Life, 37:6)

32.
FLATTERY AND DARING

Whoever has made a profound experience of God is left struck by both his holiness and his love and fascinated by both his greatness and his goodness. Teresa, before her Lord, with great simplicity passes from the wonder of his infinite transcendence to that of friendship and intimacy.
Teresa yields to his love. In love she suffers the pain of his absence. And she addresses to him a prayer built on a flattery that borders between boldness and tenderness.

Indeed, I took delight in the Lord today and dared to complain of His Majesty, and I said to Him: "How is it, my God, that it's not enough that You keep me in this miserable life and that for love of You I undergo it and desire to live where everything hinders the enjoyment of You, in that I have to eat and sleep and carry on business and talk with everyone (and I suffer all for love of You, as You well know, my Lord, because it's the greatest torment for me); how is it that when there is so little time left over to enjoy Your presence You hide from me? How is this compatible with Your mercy? How can the love You bear me allow this? I believe, Lord, that if it were possible for me to hide from You as it is for You to hide from me that the love You have for me would not suffer it; but You are with me and see me always. Don't tolerate this, my Lord! I implore You to see that it is injurious to one who loves You so much."

These and other things it occurred to me to say, while understanding first how lenient the punishment reserved for me in hell was in comparison with the place I deserved. But sometimes love becomes so foolish I don't make sense; with my whole mind I make these complaints, and the Lord puts up with it all. May so good a King be praised! We wouldn't dare say these things to earthly kings!

(Life, 37:8-9)

33.
WONDER BEFORE THE PRESENCE OF THE EUCHARIST

Teresa expresses her astonishment at seeing in the Eucharist her Majesty so veiled and humbled. She praises God in union with the angels and all of creation. This prayer reveals her joy in his presence.

When I approached to receive Communion and recalled the extraordinary majesty I had seen and considered that it was present in the Blessed Sacrament (the Lord often desires that I behold it in the host), my hair stood on end; the whole experience seemed to annihilate me. O my Lord! If You did not hide Your grandeur, who would approach so often a union of something so dirty and miserable with such great majesty! May the angels and all creatures praise You, for You so measure things in accordance with our weakness that when we rejoice in Your sovereign favors Your great power does not so frighten us that, weak and wretched people, we would not dare enjoy them.

(Life, 38:19)

34.
THE EUCHARIST AND GRATITUDE

The Eucharist. The closeness and holiness of God in Christ Jesus. Teresa lived very intensely the mystery of the Eucharist, through which she nourished and enriched her prayer. She now calls to mind recent experiences of the Eucharist which she describes with sentiments of ardent love and unspeakable humility.
Reflecting on these experiences causes her to relive them again which for their sublime character makes her feel agitated and almost carried outside of herself. Her prayer bursts forth in acts of faith, adoration, petition for graces, and of her own self-offering to him.

O wealth of the poor, how admirably You know how to sustain souls! And without their seeing such great wealth, You show it to them little by little. When I behold majesty as extraordinary as this concealed in something as small as the host, it happens afterward that I marvel at wisdom so wonderful, and I fail to know how the Lord gives me the courage or strength to approach Him. If He who has granted, and still does grant me so many favors, did not give this strength, it would be impossible to conceal the fact or resist shouting aloud about marvels so great. For what will a wretched person, like myself, who is weighed down with abominations and who has wasted his life with so little fear of God, feel when he sees he is approaching this Lord of such powerful majesty and that his Lord desires that the soul behold it? How will a mouth that has spoken so many words against this very Lord be united with that most glorious body, which abounds in purity and compassion? For the love that face shows, so beautiful in its tenderness and affability, makes the soul much more sorrowful and afflicted for not having served Him than does the majesty it beholds in Him cause it to fear. But how could I have experienced twice what I saw and am about to describe?

Certainly, my Lord and my glory, I am about to say that in some way in these great afflictions my soul feels I have done something in Your service. Alas! I don't know what I'm saying to myself, because almost without my uttering this I'm already putting it down in writing. I find I'm disturbed and somewhat outside myself since I have brought these things back to mind. If this sentiment had come from me, I might truly have said that I had done something for You, my Lord; but since there can be no good thought if You do not give it, there's no reason to be thankful to myself. I am the debtor, Lord, and You the offended one.

(Life, 38:21-22)

35.
INTERCESSION: AN ASKING OR A GIVING?

Teresa speaks about prayer of intercession. On her own she comes to the realization that her requests bear new strength. The Lord shows her that they are united to his own will, "so that we understand that He listens to us, sympathizes with our requests, and answers them." This act of asking calls within her the need to offer something of herself, or better, to give her entire self to Him.

May He be blessed forever who gives so much, and to whom I give so little. For what does he do, my Lord, who doesn't get rid of everything for You? How I fail, how I fail, how I fail—and I could say it a thousand times—to get rid of everything for You! There's no reason on this account to want to live (although there are other reasons), because I don't live in conformity with what I owe You. How many imperfections I see in myself! What laxity in serving You! Indeed I think sometimes I would like to be without consciousness in order not to know so much evil about myself. May He who is able provide the remedy.

(Life, 39:6)

36.
FORGIVE ME MY LORD

Teresa thinks it would be a petty thing to call to mind past merits or personal services in order to ask something of God. The prayer of petition rests on a foundation of another kind.
*"The years spent in prayer are to be left aside, because in all that we do we can only merit contempt in comparison to what the Lord has done for us in shedding a single drop of his blood. Now if it is true that the more we serve him, the more we become debtors to him, what does it come to our mind to expect, when for a single coin we pay toward our debt, we receive another thousand" (*Life, *39:13, 16).*

Yet pardon me, my Lord, and don't blame me for having to console myself with something, for I don't serve You in anything. If I served You in great matters, I wouldn't be paying attention to trifles. Blessed are those persons who serve You with great deeds! If it were taken into account that I envy them and desire these deeds, I wouldn't be very far behind in pleasing You; but I'm not worth anything, my Lord. Give me worth Yourself since You love me so much.

(Life, 39:13)

37.
LEAD ME OUT OF THE ABYSS OF FALSEHOOD

Saint Teresa concludes her autobiography (chapter 40) by telling of a particular interior illumination which was both simple and blinding in light. God is the highest truth "the essence of Truth, that has no beginning or end, and upon which all other truths depend in the same way that all loves derive their being from the one Love, all greatness from the one Greatness." And this truth is found reflected in the Sacred Scriptures demonstrating that all the evil of the world derives exclusively "from the fact the truths of the Sacred Scriptures are not known in their fullness" (40:1, 4). For this reason, a background of falsehood dominates the scene of this world. And also for this reason, for her the bitter saying in the psalms, "Every man is a liar," is most correct. "It seemed I was carried into and filled with that majesty I at other

times understood. Within this majesty I was given knowledge of a truth
that is the fulfillment of all truths . . ." (40:1).
She turns from this light to look to herself and exclaims:

O my Grandeur and Majesty! What are You doing, my all-powerful
Lord? Look upon whom You bestow such sovereign favors! Don't
You recall that this soul has been an abyss of lies and a sea of vanities,
and all through my own fault? For even though You gave me the
natural temperament to abhor the lie, I myself in dealing with many
things have lied. How do You bear it, my God? How is such great
consolation and favor compatible with one who so poorly deserves
this from You?

(Life, 40:4)

38.
A PRAYER FOR LIFE'S CONTINUATION

These are the last lines of The Book of Her Life. *More than narrating*
her own story, she told of God's story in her—his story of salvation.
Though the narrative has ended, her life remains without an epilogue.
Though she is full of graces, she is still exposed to all of life's dangers.
This is the reason why Teresa closes her book with this humble prayer
of petition.

May it please the Lord, since He is powerful and can hear me if He
wants, that I might succeed in doing His will in everything. May his
Majesty not allow this soul to be lost, which, with so many artifices,
in so many ways, and so often, He has rescued from hell and brought
to Himself. Amen.

(Life, 40:24)

39.
TERESA'S PRAYER WITH AND FOR THE READER

After she finished writing her life story, Saint Teresa wrote a letter to
Garcia de Toledo, a Dominican, the specific reader for whom she wrote
the book. Even the letter addressed to him concludes with a simple
prayer to God.

I shall recommend your Reverence's soul to our Lord for the rest
of my life. So do me the favor of hurrying to serve his Majesty; for
you will see, from what is written here, how well one is occupied when
one gives oneself entirely—as your Reverence has begun to do—to
Him who so immeasurably gives Himself to us.

May He be blessed forever! I hope in His mercy that your Reverence and I will see each other there where we shall behold more clearly the great things He has done for us, and praise Him for ever and ever, amen.

(Letter to Fr. Garcia de Toledo, June 1562)

A COMMUNITY OF PRAYER – *THE WAY OF PERFECTION*

This next set of prayers has been selected from Teresa's book The Way of Perfection *written for the first small group of Carmelite disciples of hers and for whom she inaugurates her spiritual teaching profession.*

The book throughout contains instruction for prayer.

In order for prayer to be Christian and life-transforming – Teresa feels – the one who prays must be open to what concerns the Church and feel the great needs of all; one must be committed to living the evangelical virtues, which include love, poverty, humility, perseverance; and one must acquire a "determined determination."

Teresa then will lead and accompany the reader in reciting the Christian prayer par excellence, the Our Father.

Teresa does not fall into the trap of not practicing what she speaks about. Her most effective teaching method, therefore, is to pray in the presence of the reader. The explanations of doctrinal subjects she treats (the Church, poverty, brotherly love, detachment, silence, determination) are not just theoretical matters to pass on, but contain her own experience of them. Each topic becomes means for a spontaneous and immediate encounter with God. How can one speak of these things without addressing Him at the same time, without summoning Him, or seeking His assistance?

This is just what Teresa does. She shifts her attention from her disciple-readers in order to pray to God in their presence and to have them join her at times because she is convinced that Christian prayer flows through mysterious channels of communication that lead to union with God.

Today's reader can also fully enroll into this spiritual school of Saint Teresa's by learning how she prays, by taking part in her prayer, and by feeling constantly encouraged to establish a personal dialogue with God.

40.
I WOULD HAVE GIVEN A THOUSAND LIVES . . .

This is the first prayer that appears in The Way of Perfection. *She precedes it with a wide panorama of the Church: the wounds that inflict it. It is the moment when the unity of the Christians in Europe is broken; religious wars become wide-spread. Teresa expresses her turmoil and prays for all Christians. "The world is burning away . . . must we waste any time?"*

At that time news reached me of the harm being done in France and of the havoc the Lutherans had caused and how much this miserable sect was growing.* The news distressed me greatly, and, as though I could do something or were something, I cried to the Lord and begged Him that I might remedy so much evil. It seemed to me that I would have given a thousand lives to save one soul out of the many that were being lost there. I realized I was a woman and wretched and incapable of doing any of the useful things I desired to do in the service of the Lord.

O my Redeemer, my heart cannot bear these thoughts without becoming terribly grieved. What is the matter with Christians nowadays? Must it always be those who owe You the most who afflict You? Those for whom You performed the greatest works, those You have chosen for Your friends, with whom You walk and consume by means of Your sacraments? Aren't they satisfied with the torments You have suffered for them?

(Way, 1:2-3)

41.
NO, MY CREATOR, YOU ARE NOT UNGRATEFUL

Teresa feels as though she were invested with a priestly power in order to pray on behalf of the Church. This is the prayer of a woman wounded by the sufferings of the Church. It is a request expressed by a community of prayer: the twelve young girls gathered in the first Carmel.

It seems bold that I think I could play some role in obtaining an answer to these petitions. I trust, my Lord, in these Your servants who

---

* This unecumenical statement by Teresa should of course be understood in the context of the time she lived in. Fortunately many initiatives within the ecumenical movement have brought members of different Christian churches closer to one another and many Christians nowadays believe in and strive for the fulfillment of Jesus' prayer "That all may be one" (Jn 17:21).

live here, and I know they desire and strive for nothing else than to please You. For You they renounced the little they had – and would have wanted to have more so as to serve You with it. Since You, my Creator, are not ungrateful, I think You will not fail to do what they beg of You. Nor did You, Lord, when You walked in the world, despise women; rather, You always, with great compassion, helped them. When we ask You for honors, income, money, or worldly things, do not hear us. But when we ask You for the honor of Your Son, why wouldn't You hear us, eternal Father, for the sake of Him who lost a thousand honors and a thousand lives for You? Not for us, Lord, for we don't deserve it, but for the blood of Your Son and His merits.

(Way, 3:7)

42.
DON'T ALLOW CHRISTIANITY ANY MORE HARM

Teresa turns to the Father in heaven. She prays to Him for the Church, in which Christ is present and humiliated in its Mystical Body. From within this Church lacerated by its own children and in so dire need of grace, Teresa becomes conscious of her own co-responsibility in all that takes place.

O eternal Father, see to it that so many lashes and injuries and such heavy torments are not forgotten! How then, my Creator, can a heart as loving as Yours allow that the deeds done by Your Son with such ardent love and so as to make us more pleasing to You (for You commanded that He love us) be esteemed so little? For nowadays these heretics have so little regard for the Blessed Sacrament that they take away its dwelling places by destroying churches. Was something still to be done to please You? But He did everything.

Wasn't it enough, eternal Father, that while He lived He did not have a place to lay His head – and always in the midst of so many trials? But now they take away the places He has at present for inviting His friends, for He realizes that we are weak and knows that the laborers must be nourished with such food. Hasn't He already paid far more than enough for the sin of Adam? Don't allow this, my Emperor! Let Your Majesty be at once appeased! Do not look at our sins but behold that Your most blessed Son redeemed us, and behold His merits and those of His glorious Mother and of so many saints and martyrs who died for You!

Ah, what a pity, Lord, and who has dared to make this petition on behalf of all of us? What a bad intermediary, my daughters, is she who seeks to be heard and to make such a petition for you! Indeed, this sovereign Judge should become more indignant – and rightly and justly so — at seeing me so bold! But behold, my Lord, that You are a God of mercy; have mercy on this little sinner, this little worm that is so bold with You. Behold, my God, my desires and the tears with which I beg this of You; forget my deeds because of who You are; have pity on so many souls that are being lost, and help Your Church. Don't allow any more harm to come to Christianity, Lord. Give light now to these darknesses.

(Way, 3:8-9)

43.
THANK YOU LORD FOR HAVING CALLED ME

Teresa thanks God for the gift of her religious vocation and for the opportunity to be among this group of young "readers" at the first Carmel of Saint Joseph's in Avila.

May You be blessed, my God, and all creatures praise You! One cannot repay You for this favor — as is likewise so for many others You have granted me — for my vocation to be a nun was a very great favor! Since I have been so miserable, You did not trust me, Lord. Instead of keeping me where there were so many living together and where my wretchedness would not have been so clearly seen during my lifetime, You have brought me to a place where, since there are so few nuns, it seems impossible for this wretchedness not to be known. That I might walk more carefully, You have removed from me all opportunities to conceal it. Now I confess there is no longer an excuse for me, Lord, and so I have greater need of Your mercy that You might pardon any fault I may have.

(Way, 8:2)

44.
GIVE ME LIGHT, FOR MY EYES ARE BLIND

Give me a desire for truth. Teresa asks God to defend her from her own self and to free her from any tendency toward wanting to prove her own innocence.

O my Lord, when I think of the many ways You suffered and how You deserved none of these sufferings, I don't know what to say about myself, nor do I know where my common sense was when I didn't want to suffer, nor where I am when I excuse myself. You already know, my Good, that if I have some good it is a gift from no one else's hands but Yours. Now, Lord, what costs You more, to give much or little? If it is true that I have not merited this good, neither have I merited the favors You have granted me. Is it possible that I have wanted anyone to feel good about a thing as bad as I after so many evil things have been said about You who are the Good above all goods? Don't allow, don't allow, my God – nor would I ever want You to allow – that there be anything in Your servant that is displeasing in Your eyes. Observe, Lord, that mine are blind and satisfied with very little. Give me light and grant that I may truly desire to be abhorred by all since I have so often failed You who have loved me so faithfully.

(Way, 15:5)

45.
FOR OBTAINING THE POWER TO REMAIN SILENT

To remain silent out of love, as Christ did on the cross.

What is this, my God? What do we expect to obtain from pleasing creatures? What does it matter if we are blamed a lot by all of them if in Your presence we are without fault? O my Sisters, we never completely understand this virtue; so, we are never completely perfect if we do not reflect and think a great deal upon what is and what is not.

However enclosed you are, never think that the good or evil you do will remain a secret. And do you think, daughters, that when you do not excuse yourselves there will be lacking someone to defend you? Observe how the Lord answered for the Magdalene both in the house of the Pharisee and when her sister accused her. He will not be as harsh with you as He was with Himself, for at the time that one of the thieves defended Him, He was on the cross.

(Way, 15:6-7)

46.
YOUR ARMS ARE STRONG, MY CRUCIFIED LORD

A confidential prayer to Jesus on the mystery of the cross, his love, his humility. She asks Him for the medicine of love, the fortune to be "healed with so soothing a balm."

O my Lord, how often do we make You fight the devil in arm to arm combat!

Isn't it enough that You allowed him to take You in his arms when he carried You to the pinnacle of the temple so that You might teach us how to conquer him? But what would it be like, daughters, to see him, with his darknesses, next to the Sun. And what fear that unfortunate one must have borne without knowing why, for God didn't allow him to understand it. Blessed be such compassion and mercy. What shame we Christians ought to have for making Him wrestle arm to arm, as I have said, with so foul a beast.

It was truly necessary, Lord, that you have such strong arms. But how is it that they didn't weaken by the many torments You suffered on the cross? Oh, how everything that is suffered with love is healed again! And so I believe that had You survived, the very love You have for us would have healed Your wounds, for no other medicine was necessary. O my God, grant that I might put medicine like this in everything that causes me pain and trial! How eagerly I would desire these if I could be sure that I'd be healed with so soothing a balm!

(Way, 16:7)

47.
KEEP OUR EYES FIXED ON YOU, O LORD

You are life.

O Lord, how true that all harm comes to us from not keeping our eyes fixed on You; if we were to look at nothing else but the way, we would soon arrive. But we meet with a thousand falls and obstacles and lose the way because we don't keep our eyes—as I say—on the true way. It seems so new to us that you would think we had never walked on it. It's certainly something to excite pity, that which sometimes happens.

(Way, 16:11)

48.
GIVE US LIVING WATER

O my Lord, and who will find himself so immersed in this living water that he will die! But, is this possible?

(Way, 19:8)

49.
DELIVER US FROM FALSEHOOD

O my Lord, defend Yourself! See how they understand Your words in reverse. Don't permit such weaknesses in Your servants.

(Way, 21:8)

50.
YOU ARE KING

Your kingdom will have no end. I praise you and bless you forever.

Well, what is this, my Lord? What is this, my Emperor? How can it be tolerated? You are King forever, my God; Your kingdom is not a borrowed one. When in the Creed the words, "and His kingdom will have no end," are said, it is almost always a special delight for me. I praise You, Lord, and bless You forever; in sum, Your kingdom will last forever. Well then, may You never permit, Lord, that anyone who is about to speak to You consider it good to do so only vocally.

(Way, 22:2)

51.
I KNOW YOU, LORD

Who can know you in depth? You are an ocean of wonders, you are the beauty that contains all beauties.

Oh, our Emperor, supreme Power, supreme Goodness, Wisdom itself, without beginning, without end, without any limit to Your works; they are infinite and incomprehensible, a fathomless sea of marvels, with a beauty containing all beauty, strength itself! Oh, God help me, who might possess here all human eloquence and wisdom together in order to know how to explain clearly — insofar as is possible here below, because in this case all knowledge is equivalent to knowing nothing — a number of the many things we can consider in order to have some knowledge of who this Lord and Good of ours is!

(Way, 22:6)

52.
SET YOUR EYES ON CHRIST

Look at him and tell him, "Let's go together, Lord."

If you are experiencing trials or are sad, behold Him on the way to the garden: what great affliction He bore in His soul; for having become suffering itself, He tells us about it and complains of it. Or behold Him bound to the column, filled with pain, with all His flesh torn in pieces for the great love He bears you; so much suffering, persecuted by some, spit on by others, denied by His friends, abandoned by them, with no one to defend Him, frozen from the cold, left so alone that you can console each other. Or behold Him burdened with the cross, for they didn't even let Him take a breath. He will look at you with those eyes so beautiful and compassionate, filled with tears; He will forget His sorrows so as to console you in yours, merely because you yourselves go to Him to be consoled, and you turn your head to look at Him.

O Lord of the world, my true Spouse! Are You so in need, my Lord and my Love, that You would want to receive such poor company as mine, for I see by Your expression that You have been consoled by me? Well then, how is it Lord that the angels leave You and that even Your Father doesn't console You?

If it's true, Lord, that You want to endure everything for me, what is this that I suffer for You? Of what am I complaining? I am already ashamed, since I have seen You in such a condition. I desire to suffer, Lord, all the trials that come to me and esteem them as a great good enabling me to imitate You in something. Let us walk together, Lord. Wherever You go, I will go; whatever you suffer, I will suffer.

(Way, 26:5-6)

53.
"OUR FATHER"

You, O God, are our Father. And you, Christ, Son of God, how can you give us such a marvelous gift in these first words of our prayer?

Our Father who art in heaven. O my Lord, how You do show Yourself to be the Father of such a Son; and how Your Son does show Himself to be the Son of such a Father! May You be blessed forever and ever! This favor would not be so great, Lord, if it came at the end of the prayer. But at the beginning, You fill our hands and give a reward so large that it would easily fill the intellect and thus occupy the will in such a way one would be unable to speak a word.

Oh, daughters, how readily should perfect contemplation come at this point! Oh, how right it would be for the soul to enter within itself in order to rise the better above itself that this holy Son might make it understand the nature of the place where He says His Father dwells, which is in the heavens. Let us go forth from the earth, my daughters, for there is no reason that a favor like this should be so little esteemed, that after we have understood how great it is, we should still want to remain on earth.

O Son of God and my Lord! How is it that You give so much all together in the first words? Since You humble Yourself to such an extreme in joining with us in prayer and making Yourself the Brother of creatures so lowly and wretched, how is it that You give us in the name of Your Father everything that can be given? For you desire that

He consider us His children, because Your word cannot fail. You oblige Him to be true to Your word, which is no small burden since in being Father He must bear with us no matter how serious the offenses. If we return to Him like the prodigal son, He has to pardon us. He has to console us in our trials. He has to sustain us in the way a father like this must. For, in effect, He must be better than all the fathers in the world because in Him everything must be faultless. And after all this He must make us sharers and heirs with You.

Behold, my Lord, that since with the love You bear us and with Your humility, nothing will stop you . . . in sum, Lord, You are on earth and clothed with it. Since You possess our nature, it seems You have some reason to look to our gain. But behold, Your Father is in heaven. You Yourself said so. It is right that You look to His honor. Since You have vowed to undergo disgrace for us, leave Your Father free. Don't oblige Him to do so much for a people so wretched, like myself, who will not thank You properly.

(Way, 27:1, 2, 3)

54.
"WHO ART IN HEAVEN"

You who lie in the depths of my being . . .

Now consider what your master says: Who art in heaven. Do you think it's of little importance to know what heaven is and where you must seek your most sacred Father? Well, I tell you that for wandering minds it is very important not only to believe these truths but to strive to understand them by experience. Doing this is one of the ways of greatly slowing down the mind and recollecting the soul.

You already know that God is everywhere. It's obvious, then, that where the king is there is his court; in sum, wherever God is, there is heaven. Without a doubt you can believe that where His Majesty is present, all glory is present. Consider what St. Augustine says, that he sought Him in many places but found Him ultimately within himself. Do you think it matters little for a soul with a wandering mind to understand this truth and see that there is no need to go to heaven in order to speak with one's Eternal Father or find delight in Him? Nor is there any need to shout. However softly we speak, He is near enough to hear us. Neither is there any need for wings to go to find Him. All one need do is go into solitude and look at Him within oneself, and not turn away from so good a Guest but with great humility speak to Him as to a father. Beseech Him as you would a father; tell Him about your trials; ask Him for a remedy against them, realizing that you are not worthy to be His daughter.

(Way, 28:1-2)

55.

O ETERNAL WISDOM

"Your kingdom come."

Couldn't You, my Lord, have concluded the Our Father with the words: "Give us, Father, what is fitting for us"? It doesn't seem there would have been need to say anything else to One who understands everything so well.

O Eternal Wisdom! Between You and Your Father these words would have sufficed. Your petition in the garden was like this. You manifested Your own desire and fear, but You abandoned them to His will. Yet, You know us, my Lord, that we are not as surrendered to the will of Your Father as You were. You know that it was necessary for You to make those specific requests so that we might pause to consider if what we are seeking is good for us, so that if it isn't we won't ask for it. If we aren't given what we want, being what we are, with this free will we have, we might not accept what the Lord gives. For although what He gives is better, we don't think we'll ever become rich, since we don't at once see the money in our hand.

(Way, 30:1-2)

56.

"YOUR WILL BE DONE"

That the earth may be your heaven.

"Your will be done on earth as it is in heaven." You did well, good Master of ours, to make this petition so that we might accomplish what You give on our behalf. For certainly, Lord, if You hadn't made the petition, the task would seem to me impossible. But when Your Father does what You ask Him by giving us His kingdom here on earth, I know that we shall make Your words come true by giving what You give for us. For once the earth has become heaven, the possibility is there for Your will to be done in me. But if the earth hasn't — and earth as wretched and barren as mine — I don't know, Lord, how it will be possible. It is indeed a great thing, that which You offer!

(Way, 32:2)

57.
"HALLOWED BE YOUR NAME"

I give you my will. Be glorified in me.

Now let me put it in another way. Look, daughters, His will must be done whether we like this or not, and it will be done in heaven and on earth. Believe me, take my advice, and make a virtue of necessity. O my Lord, what a great comfort this is for me, that you didn't want the fulfillment of Your will to depend on a will as wretched as mine! May You be blessed forever, and may all things praise You! Your name be glorified forever! I'd be in a fine state, Lord, if it were up to me as to whether or not Your will were to be done! Now I freely give mine to You, even though I do so at a time in which I'm not free of self-interest. For I have felt and have had great experience of the gain that comes from freely abandoning my will to Yours. O friends, what a great gain there is here! Oh, what a great loss there is when we do not carry out what we offer to the Lord in the Our Father!

(*Way,* 32:4)

58.
RECITING THE PRAYER OF JESUS

I will not turn my eyes away from you. . . . Father, may your will be done.

Fiat voluntas tua: Your will, Lord, be done in me in every way and manner that You, my Lord, want. If You want it to be done with trials, strengthen me and let them come; if with persecutions, illnesses, dishonors, and a lack of life's necessities, here I am; I will not turn away, my Father, nor is it right that I turn my back on You. Since Your-Son gave You this will of mine in the name of all, there's no reason for any lack on my part. But grant me the favor of Your kingdom that I may do Your will, since He asked for this kingdom for me, and use me as You would Your own possession, in conformity with Your will.

O my Sisters, what strength lies in this gift! It does nothing less, when accompanied by the necessary determination, than draw the Almighty so that He becomes one with our lowliness, transforms us into Himself, and effects a union of the Creator with the creature. Behold whether or not you are well paid and have a good Master; since He knows how the love of His Father can be obtained, He teaches us how and by what means we must serve Him.

(*Way,* 32:10-11)

59.
OUR DAILY BREAD

Father, how can you have allowed such a great thing to be done? Prayer of admiration of the gift of the Eucharist.

Oh, God help me, what great love from the Son and what great love from the Father! Yet I am not so surprised about Jesus, for since He had already said, *fiat voluntas tua,* He had to do that will, being who He is. Yes, for He is not like us! Since, then, He knows that He does it by loving us as Himself, He went about looking for ways of doing it with greater perfection, even though His fulfillment of this commandment was at a cost to Himself. But You, Eternal Father, how is it that You consented? Why do You desire to see Your Son every day in such wretched hands? Since You have already desired to see Him in these hands and given Your consent, You have seen how they treated Him. How can You in Your compassion now see Him insulted day after day? And how many insults will be committed today against this Most Blessed Sacrament! In how many enemies' hands must the Father see Him! How much irreverence from these heretics!

O eternal Lord! Why do You accept such a petition? Why do You consent to it? Don't look at His love for us, because in exchange for doing Your will perfectly, and doing it for us, He allows Himself to be crushed to pieces each day. It is for You, my Lord, to look after Him, since He will let nothing deter Him. Why must all our good come at His expense? Why does He remain silent before all and not know how to speak for Himself, but only for us? Well, shouldn't there be someone to speak for this most loving Lamb?

(Way, 33:3-4)

60.
BEFORE THE EUCHARIST

That the Lord of the Most Holy Sacrament be not mistreated. The setting that provokes Teresa's prayer is the gloomy situation of the Church of her century that finds division and opposition regarding faith in the Eucharist.

Well, holy Father in heaven, since You desire and accept this work, and it is clear that You will not deny us anything that is good for us, there has to be someone, as I said in the beginning, who will speak for Your Son since He never looks out for Himself.

Let us be the ones, daughters, even though the thought is a bold one, we being who we are. But obeying and trusting in the Lord's command to us that we ask, let us beseech His Majesty in the name of Jesus that, since nothing remained for Him to do and He left sinners a gift as great as this one, He might in His compassion desire and be pleased to provide a remedy that His Son may not be this badly treated. Let us beseech Him that, since His Son provided a means so good that we may offer Him many times in sacrifice, this precious gift may avail; that there'll be no advance made in the very great evil and disrespect committed and shown in places where this most Blessed Sacrament is present among those Lutherans, where churches are destroyed, so many priests lost, and the sacraments taken away.

(Way, 35:3)

61.
SQUELCH THIS FIRE, LORD,
YOU WHO CAN DO WHATEVER YOU WISH

A priestly prayer, centered in the Eucharist, in view of the harm the Church suffers due to its involvement in bloody religious wars.

Well, what is this, my Lord and my God! Either bring the world to an end or provide a remedy for these very serious evils. There is no heart that can suffer them, not even among those of us who are wretched. I beseech You, Eternal Father, that You suffer them no longer. Stop this fire, Lord, for if You will You can. Behold that Your Son is still in the world. Through His reverence may all these ugly and abominable and filthy things cease. In His beauty and purity He doesn't deserve to be in a house where there are things of this sort. Do not answer for our sakes, Lord; we do not deserve it. Do it for Your Son's sake. We don't dare beseech You that He be not present with us; what would become of us? For if something appeases You, it is having a loved one like this here below. Since some means must be had, my Lord, may Your Majesty provide it.

(Way, 35:4)

62.
DO SOMETHING TO CALM THESE WATERS

Prayer of intercession for the entire world and for the Church: we offer you, Father, the most sacred Bread which you have given to us.

O my God, would that I might have begged You much and served You diligently so as to be able to ask for this great favor in payment for my services, since You don't leave anyone without pay! But I have not done so, Lord; rather, perhaps I am the one who has angered You so that my sins have caused these many evils to come about. Well, what is there for me to do, my Creator, but offer this most blessed bread to You, and even though You have given it to us, return it to You and beg You through the merits of Your Son to grant me this favor since in so many ways He has merited that You do so? Now, Lord, now; make the sea calm! May this ship, which is the Church, not always have to journey in a tempest like this. Save us, Lord, for we are perishing.

(Way, 35:5)

63.
FORGIVE US, LORD, IN THE MEASURE THAT WE FORGIVE OTHERS

Teach us to forgive as you forgive.

Forgive us our sins, as we forgive those who sin against us.

But, my Lord, are there some persons in my company who have not understood this? If there are, I beg them in Your name to remember this and pay no attention to the little things they call wrongs. It seems that, like children, we are making houses out of straw with these ceremonious little rules of etiquette. Oh, God help me, Sisters, if we knew what honor is and what losing honor consists in!

O Lord, Lord! Are You our Model and Master? Yes, indeed! Well then, what did Your honor consist of, You who honored us? Didn't you indeed lose it in being humiliated unto death? No, Lord, but You won it for all.

(Way, 36:3, 5)

64.
FORGIVE ME, LORD, EVEN THOUGH I FIND NOTHING IN OTHERS THAT NEEDS MY FORGIVENESS

May Your name be blessed for all eternity. Amen. Through such a name I now beg the Eternal Father to forgive my debts and my great sins. Though I have never had reason to have to forgive others on their account, I myself have much each day to be forgiven. And may He grant me the grace that one day I be in the position to have something to offer as a backing for something to request.

(Way, E 65:3)

65.
DO NOT ALLOW US TO FALL

Take away our journey's fears.

Thus, Eternal Father, what can we do but have recourse to You and pray that these enemies of ours not lead us into temptation? Let public enemies come, for by Your favor we will be more easily freed. But these other treacheries; who will understand them, my God? We always need to pray to You for a remedy. Instruct us, Lord, so that we may understand ourselves and be secure. You already know that few take this path; but if they have to travel it with so many fears, many fewer will take it.

(Way, 39:6)

66.
LORD, GIVE ME AN AUTHENTIC LOVE

"Do not allow me to leave this life without having obtained it."

How much I have gone on to write! Yet it is not as much as I would have liked to. If it is gratifying just to speak about the love of God, what would it be like to possess it? O my Lord, give me this love! Allow me, at least, to not leave this life until I have learned to relinquish every desire for created things, to want nothing else but to love You, and to avoid replacing the treasure of love with anything else, because here below everything is false, for since the foundations are erroneous, the rest of the structure cannot stand secure.

(Way, E 71:1)

67.
LORD, FREE US FROM ALL EVIL

I cannot bear "not knowing with certainty whether I love you!"

Deliver me, Lord, from this shadow of death! Deliver me from these many afflictions, deliver me from these many sorrows, deliver me from these many flighty and freakish occurrences. Deliver me from all the ceremonial formalities which we have to put up with here below! Deliver me from the many, many bureaucratic ways that tire and annoy me, and if I had to list them all I would bore my readers to death! At this point I feel as though it is no longer possible to live here on earth. This state of exhaustion must have come from the fact that I have lived very poorly, and no less from the realization that not even my present living is based on an authentic life, for I am in great debt.

O my Lord, deliver me from all evil, and deign Yourself to lead me where all goodness is found.

(Way, E 72:4)

68.
PRAYER OF HOPE

"What can we hope for here? After presenting our requests to the Almighty, let's allow him the freedom to give us what he wills." This is the concluding prayer in Teresa's book The Way of Perfection. *It is her commentary on the "Amen" in her meditation on the Our Father. In a delicate way, her own prayer becomes the prayer of the community and ends with a final blessing.*

What do they still hope for here, those to whom You have given knowledge of what the world is, and those who have a living faith concerning what the Eternal Father has kept for them?

Oh, how different this life would have to be in order for one not to desire death! How our will deviates in its inclination from that which is the will of God. He wants us to love truth; we love the lie. He wants us to desire the eternal; we, here below, lean toward what comes to an end. He wants us to desire sublime and great things; we, here below, desire base and earthly things. He would want us to desire only what is secure; we, here below, love the dubious.

Everything is a mockery, my daughters, except beseeching God to free us from these dangers forever and draw us at last away from every evil.

Even though our desire may not be perfect, let us force ourselves to make the request. What does it cost us to ask for a great deal? We are asking it of One who is powerful.

But in order to be right, let us leave the giving to His will since we have already given Him our own. His name be forever hallowed in heaven and on earth, and may His will be always done in me. Amen.

(Way, 42:2, 4)

PRAYERS FROM
MEDITATIONS ON THE SONG OF SONGS

The next set of prayers has been chosen from a brief commentary of Teresa's on the Song of Songs. It took great boldness on her part to comment on such a biblical book considering the spiritual atmosphere of her time. Though on the whole her commentary amounted to a limited number of verses, they were soon to be burned. Enough of their fragments, however, were left intact to allow us to participate in this privileged aspect of her prayer: her encounter with the words of Scripture as a means to her elevation to God.

In her writing, though remaining anonymous, Teresa reveals the following personal reflection: "I know someone who has lived for years in all kinds of fears, without even being able to find any reassurance, until she fell upon — so the Lord permitted — several passages of the Song of Songs, which gave her the understanding that she was on the right path. In fact, she understood how it were possible for a soul in love with her Spouse to experience these pleasures, swoons, deaths and afflictions, delights and joys with Him, after having left those of the world out of love for Him, and having entirely given up and abandoned oneself in His hands, not only in word, as has happened to someone, but in truth, proven in works" (Meditations, 1:6).

Later, in one of her poems, she will celebrate the festivity of the Song of Songs, explaining the key phrase of the book, "My lover belongs to me, and I to him" (Sg 2:16).

"Look to the one who looks upon you" (God or Christ) is one of the typical instructions of a contemplative as her. Fixing her eyes on Him is one of her personal experiences, a millstone on which she shapes her teaching on Christian prayer: "These two lovers look directly into each other's eyes" (Life, 27:10). The following prayers emerge from the depths of contemplation and from the fire of this kind of love. It is the interest also of many today — we ourselves — to draw closer to the fire of the biblical word and mystical prayer.

69.
THE LANGUAGE OF LOVE

To the Holy Spirit she says, "A word of yours contains a thousand mysteries." We, on the other hand, are "inexperienced in loving you."

O my Lord, how poorly we profit from the blessing You grant us! You seek ways and means and you devise plans to show Your love for us; we, inexperienced in loving You, esteem this love so poorly that our minds, little exercised in love, go where they always go and cease to think of the great mysteries this language, spoken by the Holy Spirit, contains within itself.

Let Him kiss me with the kiss of His mouth O my Lord and my God, and what words are these that a worm speaks them to its Creator! May You be blessed, Lord, for in so many ways have You taught us! But who will dare, my King, utter these words without Your permission?

(Meditations, 1:4, 10)

70.
PEACE AND FRIENDSHIP

Teresa speaks of reciting verses of the Song of Songs in the presence of the Eucharist or out of the boldness of love.

How much majesty You bear, my Lord, in the most Blessed Sacrament. But since these persons do not have a living faith but a dead one, You do not speak to them when they see You so humble under the species of bread. They do not deserve to hear — and they are not so daring.

As a result these words in themselves, taking them only literally, would truly cause fear if the one uttering them were in his senses. But the one whom Your love, Lord, has drawn out of himself, You will truly pardon if he says them and also others, even though to say them is daring. And my Lord, if the kiss signifies peace and friendship why shouldn't souls ask You for this kiss? What better thing can we ask for than what I ask You for, my Lord; that You give me this peace "with the kiss of Your mouth"?

(Meditations, 1:11, 12)

71.
HAVE YOU FORGOTTEN YOUR GREATNESS?

May You be blessed, Lord, my God, for You show us so much pity

that it seems You forget Your greatness so as not to punish — as would
be right — a betrayal as treacherous as this.

(Meditations, 2:10)

72.
WORDS THAT WOUND THE SOUL WITH LOVE

"In the Song of Songs the Lord himself incites us to pronounce them."

O Lord of heaven and earth, how is it possible that even while in
this mortal life one can enjoy You with so special a friendship, that
the Holy Spirit says this so clearly in these words, and that still we do
not want to understand that these are the delights You share with souls
in this Song of Songs! What endearing words! What sweetness! One
of these words would have been enough for us to be dissolved in You.
May You be blessed, Lord, because we don't lose anything through
Your fault. Along how many paths, in how many ways, by how many
methods You show us love! With trials, with a death so harsh, with
torments, suffering offenses every day and then pardoning; and not
only with these deeds do You show this love, but with words so capable
of wounding the soul in love with You that You say them in this Song
of Songs and teach the soul what to say to You. For I don't know how
the words can be endured if You do not help the one who hears them
to bear them — because of our weakness, not because of what the words
deserve.

(Meditations, 3:14)

73.
UNITE MY WILL TO YOURS

"That nothing may keep me from declaring you my love."

Hence, my Lord, I do not ask You for anything else in life but that
You kiss me with the kiss of Your mouth, and that You do so in such
a way that although I may want to withdraw from this friendship and
union, my will may always, Lord of my life, be subject to Your will
and not depart from it; that there be nothing to impede me from being
able to say: "My God and my Glory, indeed Your breasts are better
and more delightful than wine."

(Meditations, 3:15)

74.
THE WINE YOU GIVE ME IS PRECIOUS

"A drop alone of your love is worth more than all of creation." Teresa comments on the verse of the Song of Songs: "Your breasts are better than wine."

Great is this favor, my Spouse; a pleasing feast. Precious wine do You give me, for with one drop alone You make me forget all of creation and go out from creatures and myself, so that I will no longer want the joys and comforts that my sensuality desired up until now. Great is this favor; I did not deserve it.

(Meditations, 4:6)

75.
MY DELIGHT

"My Beloved belongs to me and I to my Beloved. What is his is mine and what is mine his."

O my Jesus, who could explain the benefit that lies in throwing ourselves into the arms of this Lord of ours and making an agreement with His Majesty that I look at my Beloved, and my Beloved at me, and that He look after my things and I look after His! Let's not, as the saying goes, love ourselves to death. I repeat, my God, and beg You through the blood of your Son that You grant me this favor: Let Him kiss me with the kiss of His mouth, for without You, what am I, Lord? If I am not close to You, what am I worth? If I stray a little from Your Majesty, where will I end up?

(Meditations, 4:8)

76.
GIVE ME WHAT YOU COMMAND
AND COMMAND WHAT YOU WILL

Oh, my Lord, my Mercy, and my Good! And what greater good could I want in this life than to be close to You that there be no division between You and me? With this companionship, what can be difficult? What can one not undertake for You, being so closely joined? What is there in me to be grateful for, my Lord? Rather, I must blame myself very much for my failure to serve You. And thus I beg You, with St. Augustine, and with full determination, that You "give me what You command and command what You will." Never, with Your favor and help, will I turn my back on You.

(Meditations, 4:9)

77.
A DIALOGUE OF LOVE

Things that only love dares to say.

Now I see, my Bridegroom, that You are mine. I cannot deny it. You came into the world for me; for me You underwent severe trials; for me You suffered many lashes; for me You remain in the most Blessed Sacrament; and now you grant me so many wonderful favors. How can I be Yours, my God? What can one who has used so unskillfully the favors You have granted to do for You? What can be expected of her services? Since with Your help she does something, consider what a poor worm will be able to do. Why does a Lord so powerful need her?

Oh, love! How I would want to say this word everywhere because love alone is that which can dare say with the bride, I am my Beloved's. He gives us permission to think that He, this true Lover, my Spouse and my Good, needs us. Since He gives us permission, let us repeat, daughters, my Beloved is mine and I am my Beloved's. You are mine, Lord? If You come to me, why do I doubt that I will be able to serve You? From here on, Lord, I want to forget myself and look only at how I can serve You and have no other desire than to do Your will.

But my desire is not powerful, my God; You are the powerful One. What I can do is be determined; thus from this very moment I am determined to serve You through deeds.

(Meditations, 4:10, 11, 12)

78.
LORD, YOU ARE SO GOOD A LOVER

"I delight to rest in his shadow, and his fruit is sweet to my mouth."

O Lord, how great are these mercies You show to the soul here! May You be blessed and praised forever, for You are so good a Lover. O my God and my Creator! Is it possible that there is no one who loves You? Oh, alas, and how often it is I who do not love You! Why didn't I merit to know You? How low do the branches of this divine apple tree reach, so that at times the soul may take hold of them by reflecting upon the grandeurs and multitude of mercies shown to it, and that it might see and enjoy the fruit that Jesus Christ, our Lord, drew from His Passion, watering this tree with His precious blood, with so admirable a love.

(Meditations, 5:5)

79.
YOUR GIFTS ARE FAR GREATER THAN OUR DESIRES

Oh, God help me, how little we desire to reach Your grandeurs, Lord! How miserable we would remain if Your giving were in conformity with our asking!

(Meditations, 5:6)

80.
AS IN THE VIRGIN MARY

"He sets charity in order within me."

O Blessed Lady, how perfectly we can apply to you what takes place between God and the bride according to what is said in the Song of Songs.

O soul, beloved of God! Do not be anxious when His Majesty brings you here and speaks so endearingly; as you will see in many words that He says to the bride in the Song of Songs, such as: You are all beautiful, my love, and many others, as I say. By these He shows He is happy with her. Thus you should believe that He will not consent to your being displeasing to Him at that time, but He will help you in what you might not have known so that He may be more pleased with you.

Who is this that is as bright as the sun? O true King, and how right the bride was in giving You this name! For in a moment You can give riches and place them in a soul that they can be enjoyed forever. How well ordered love is in this soul!

(Meditations, 6:8, 9, 11)

81.
"FLOWERS AND HONEY"

My love for you continues to grow.

The King set charity in order within me, set it in order so well that the love the soul had for the world is taken away; the soul's love of itself turns to disregard; its love for its relatives is such that it loves them solely for God; its love for its neighbors and its enemies is unbelievable unless experienced — a very strong love; its love of God is boundless, for sometimes the love impels it so much that its lowly nature cannot endure the love. And since the soul sees that it is now growing weak and about to die, it says: Sustain me with flowers; surround me with apples for I am dying with the sickness of love.

(Meditations, 6:13)

PRAYERS TAKEN FROM
THE BOOK OF HER FOUNDATIONS

Gracian, a member of Teresa's caravan, spoke about the manner in which the saintly Mother traveled. "Whether lodging at the inns or riding the wagons through the streets, they always brought their convent bell along, and right on schedule they would ring the bell that called for silence and for prayer as though they were in the monastery. You would have to see with what care Mother treated the others in all aspects of the trips, as if her mind were occupied by nothing else, as if for her whole life she had been a mule-driver. She often accompanied those of the group who traveled on foot, consoling them and engaging in conversation with them. . . . At other times she spoke of the things of God, especially when traveling by mule, which she knew very well how to manage and control, making the ride feel as steady as being in a carriage." The first biographer of Saint Teresa, Francisco de Ribera, provides us with the following details: "They traveled on wagons that were well covered, and as they passed through the streets they carried on their lives inside as though they were still in the monastery. They always brought their bell with them and rang it on schedule for silence and prayer as though they were home. They even brought an hour-glass with them to clock the time. All those who traveled with the Sisters, whether priests, clerics, laypersons, or young lads, were also required to keep silence in those time periods and they too benefited from it. You would have to see the joy of those lads when the bell sounded to signal the end of the silence period. Teresa made sure to give them all something extra to eat, because they kept the silence well."

Mother Teresa wrote The Book of Her Foundations *in order to record and communicate the details of her travels. The prayers she writes are not the ones born in the moments of silence. She writes of the events of her travels, and while doing so, relives them. This is the source of the spontaneous prayers in her book, prayers that would be similar to those experienced within the wagons or in contemplating the ever new panoramas of the countryside. A companion of her journey, Maria de San José writes:*

"On the first day, at about the hour for rest, we arrived at a beautiful forest, which we could hardly keep our holy Mother away from because the variety of its flowers and the numerous birdsongs

had directed all her attention to praising God. We spent the night in a hermitage dedicated to Saint Andrew, which was situated just below the town of Santisteban. We prayed and rested throughout the night on the cold and hard slabs of the church, uncomfortably though happily. We bore our burdens in a state of laughter to the point of even composing ballads and songs about all the things that happened to us. Our good Mother enjoyed them so much that she repeatedly thanked us for tolerating the many discomforts cheerfully and joyfully" (Book of Recreations, 9).

Here is a sample of the prayers that characterized such a wandering school.

82.
YOU GIVE BOLDNESS TO AN ANT

Though she has not yet begun to travel and set up new monasteries, she has already received the investiture of a foundress. An inner voice told her: "You will do great things." Before taking up her first journey, Teresa, in deep thought, turns to God:

O greatness of God! How You manifest Your power in giving courage to an ant! How true, my Lord, that it is not because of You that those who love You fail to do great works but because of our own cowardice and pusillanimity. . . . Who is more fond than You of giving, or of serving even at a cost to Yourself, when there is someone open to receive?

(Foundations, 2:7)

83.
WHEN WE DON'T TEND TOWARD ANYTHING ELSE BUT YOU

Teresa draws a balance on the graces which God had showered upon the pioneers of her foundations: "In the moment that these dove-cots of the Blessed Virgin began to be filled, His Majesty began to manifest his greatness in the little women gathered there, weak by nature, though strong in desire. . . . " Teresa confides in Him:

Since, my Lord, we see that You often free us from the dangers in which we place ourselves, even in opposition to You, how can one believe that You will fail to free us when we aim after nothing more than to please You and delight in You? Never can I believe this!

(Foundations, 4:4)

84.
IT'S MY FAULT

The prayer of a foundress who is responsible for a group of Sisters and their future. Overwhelmed by sentiments of humility she says:

Oh, God help me! What twisted excuses and what obvious deceit! I regret, my God, to be so wretched and so useless in your service; but I know well that the fault lies within me that You do not grant me the favors You did to my forebears. I grieve over my life, Lord, when I compare it with theirs, and I cannot say this without tears. I see that I have lost what they have worked for and that I can in no way blame You.

(Foundations, 4:7)

85.
"YOUR WAY . . . YOUR HANDS . . . YOUR SERVICE"

O Lord, how different are your paths from our clumsy imaginings! And how from a soul that is already determined to love You and is abandoned into Your hands, You do not want anything but that it obey, that it inquire well into what is for Your greater service, and that it desire this! There's no need for it to be seeking out paths or choosing them, for its will is Yours. You, my Lord, take up this care of guiding it to where it receives the most benefit.

(Foundations, 5:6)

86.
OPEN THE EYES OF PARENTS, MY GOD

Valladolid. Casilda de Padilla escapes home to enter the recently founded Carmel. Her mother supports her decision, but she finds opposition on the part of her fiancé and the rest of her family. Saint Teresa prays for them:

O Lord! What a great favor You grant to those children whose parents love them so much as to want them to possess their estates, inheritance, and riches in that blessed life that has no end! . . . Open the eyes of parents, my God. Make them understand the kind of love they are obliged to have for their children so that they do not do these children so much wrong and are not complained about before God in that final judgment where, even though they may not want to know it, the value of each thing will be understood.

(Foundations, 10:9)

87.
YOUR COAT OF ARMS ARE YOUR FIVE WOUNDS

The society of that time, as in our own, imposes the tyranny of its ways: recognition, the cult of reputation, rank of nobility. Teresa cannot tolerate this way of life. She turns to Christ to ask what his title and riches consist of:

O Son of the Eternal Father, Jesus Christ, our Lord, true King of all! What did You leave in the world? What could we, your descendants, inherit from You? What did You possess, my Lord, but trials, sufferings, and dishonors? You had nothing but a wooden beam on which to swallow the painfully difficult drink of death. In sum, my

God, it does not fit those of us who want to be your true children, and hold on to their inheritance, to flee suffering. Your heraldry consists of five wounds.

(Foundations, 10:11)

88.
BE ETERNALLY GLORIFIED, MY GOD

Beas (Andalucia). The foundress interrupts her thoughts that concern a vocation at its beginnings and bursts into a blessing:

May You be blessed forever and ever, my God, for within a moment You undo a soul and remake it. What is this, Lord? I would want to ask here what the apostles asked You when You cured the blindman, whether it was his parents who had sinned. . . . Oh, great are Your judgments, Lord! You know what You are doing, but I do not know what I am saying since Your works and judgments are incomprehensible. May You be ever glorified, for You have the power to do even more. What would become of me if this were not so? . . . Sometimes I think You grant similar favors to those who love You, and You do them so much good that You give them that by which they may serve You.

(Foundations, 22:7)

89.
WHAT FEARFUL MOMENTS I LIVED THROUGH

Seville. Teresa calls to mind her anguishes and fears while journeying and lodging the nights in broken-down houses. Then, the distress and hardships of her present foundation. She speaks to the Lord about these fears.

O Jesus! How many fears I have suffered before taking possession of these foundations! I reflect on the fact that if one can feel so much fear in doing something good, for the service of God, what must be the fear of those who do evil, deeds that are against God and against neighbor? I don't know what they can gain or what satisfaction they can find as a counterbalance to all that fear.

(Foundations, 25:8)

90.
YOUR WORDS ARE DIFFERENT

Palencia. This prayer is preceded by a dialogue between Teresa and her Lord: "What are you afraid of? When have I not been there for you? What I have been in the past I am still now. . . . " Teresa answers:

O great God! How different are your words from those of men!

(*Foundations,* 29:6)

91.
YOU PAY BACK IMMEDIATELY

Burgos. A final compliment to God, her Friend, for this latest and wearisome foundation. You are a God who pays our love with tribulations!

O my Lord, how certain it is that anyone who renders You some service soon pays with a great trial! And what a precious reward a trial is for those who truly love you if we could at once understand its value!

(*Foundations,* 31:22)

SAINT TERESA'S BOOK OF PSALMS – *SOLILOQUIES*

In The Book of Her Life, *Saint Teresa relates that at times strong impulses of praise burst forth from the depths of her soul: desires to praise God "with a loud voice"; or to shout out to people caught up in trivial matters so that they might "understand the truth."*

"One would want to be living right in the midst of the world so as to be an influence for even one other person to praise God more. A woman in this state of soul would be afflicted in seeing that her own nature would impede her from doing so, and thus be envious of those who have the freedom to cry out and make known to others who this great God of hosts is" (Castle *VI:6, 3*).

Teresa died without fulfilling this desire. According to her own statements, two elements were of constant hindrance to accomplishing this; one, that she was a woman, and two, that she was a cloistered religious: "I would have otherwise done great things."

The seventeen Soliloquies, *published under this title by Brother Luis de Leon, were Teresa's escape valve. They are called "Soliloquies" because each one denotes this sense of crying out, though not with a voice that projects itself outward, but an interior impulse directed toward the deepest part of herself or toward the sphere of God and transcendence.*

The motive for each soliloquy is usually an aspect of an interior mystery she lives: life, death, the rage of sin, lost time, communion with God, expectation of a more fuller life, Christ. . . .

At the center of each soliloquy there is generally some reference to biblical phrases. "My God and my mercy," "come to me," "the lives of men are like grass that withers," "he bought us at a great price," "to appear before you dressed as a bride," "what is most necessary is to love," "you declared that your joy is to stay amongst the sons of men," "O living founts of the wounds of my God." Often these are the same words that previously shaped her Christian experience, and now they nourish her contemplation.

Therefore, the reader who encounters these soliloquies and tries to associate oneself to the writer who speaks them, finds oneself to be also before the great incentives to Christian prayer: the mystery of one's own life, of life's end, salvation history, the words of Scripture.

We decided to formulate an introduction to each of the "Soliloquies" so as to allow the reader to penetrate more easily the rich prayers and insights that Teresa left us.

92.
FIRST SOLILOQUY
ON THE MYSTERY OF HER OWN LIFE

Teresa's prayer begins precisely in the form of a soliloquy. It is an interior monologue, a cry directed at her own life: "O life, how can you survive if drawn away from your Life!"
But the most intimate region of her soul is inhabited by God. Her prayer immediately erupts into an intense dialogue with him: "O Lord, how gentle are your ways" (n. 1). "O Mercy, your works are holy and just . . . " (n. 2). "My Father and Creator, why do I cry out to you if I can find you within me" (n. 3). She concludes by placing herself once again before the mystery of her own life: "O life, who will love you, given that you are so uncertain and exposed to danger?" (n. 3).
Teresa has already faced up to the mystery of her own life many times. She has dedicated an entire book to it. She called it "The Book of God's Mercies." It allowed her to confess her wretchedness before God and before people and for which wretchedness God had forgiven her beyond measure. Since that moment, life itself provides her an incentive to prayer, a stairway to the heights of praise for God and intercessory prayer, and an inexhaustible source of desires. Desires and expectations that become prayer.
In the mystery of life and in front of the mystery of God, Teresa encounters the dual sting of solitude and absence: she finds herself "alone" before Him, and lives life "drawn away from Life." She senses that all these ways are prepared by Him; they are "sweet ways." She sees that she herself is a work of his divine hands, and that "immeasurable greatness" have operated within her.
She comes to know herself as she experiences her lowliness in looking to His greatness and to the gifts He made her a bearer.
She discovers and experiences "with all certainty that He is within me," that in the end, solitude is not solitude, nor is absence a veil to faith, nor is life itself distant from the source of life.
The Soliloquies *are full of praises, and reveal her strong awareness of God marked by her desires, though void of any arrogance and possessiveness. Teresa continues to need "certainty" in order to live. She humbly asks for this from the only One who can grant it to her.*

1. O life, life! How can you endure being separated from your Life? In so much solitude, with what are you occupied? What are you doing, since all your works are imperfect and faulty? What consoles you, O my soul, in this stormy sea? I pity myself, and have greater pity for the time I lived without pity. O Lord, how gentle are Your ways! But who will walk them without fear? I fear to live without serving You;

and when I set out to serve You, I find nothing that proves a satisfactory payment for anything of what I owe. It seems I want to be completely occupied in Your service, and when I consider well my own misery I see I can do nothing good, unless You give me this good.

2. O my God and my Mercy! What shall I do so as not to undo the great things You've done for me? Your works are holy, they are just, they are priceless and done with great wisdom, since You, Lord are wisdom itself. If my intellect busies itself with this wisdom, my will complains. It wouldn't want anything to hinder it from loving You, because the intellect cannot reach the sublime grandeurs of its God. And my will desires to enjoy Him, but it doesn't see how it can since it is placed in a prison as painful as is this mortality. Everything hinders my will, although it was helped by the consideration of your grandeurs, by which my countless miseries are better revealed.

3. Why have I said this, my God? To whom am I complaining? Who hears me but You, my Father and Creator? That You might hear of my sorrow, what need have I to speak, for I so clearly see that You are within me? This is foolish of me. But, alas, my God, how can I know for certain I'm not separated from You? O my life, how can you live with such little assurance of something so important? Who will desire you, since the gain one can acquire or hope for from you, that is, to please God in all, is so uncertain and full of dangers?

93.
SECOND SOLILOQUY
POWERFUL LOVE OF GOD

Like Saint Paul or Saint Francis of Assisi, Teresa is a Christian who has taken delight in the love of God, the love with which He nourishes His creatures and which she has transformed into an unquenchable movement toward prayer. At times, astonished before the simple fact of knowing that He loves her ("someone like me!"), she pronounced her thanks. She praised him, blessed him, and flattered him in every kind of way! She desired to love him with a love as strong as the one he gave to her. In this present soliloquy it is this love—the one of Teresa's for God—that is transformed into prayer.

Teresa pauses a moment as she finds herself before the mystery of her own love for Christ. She begins a dialogue with him, as if to awaken and incite him: "O powerful love of God!" (n. 1). She then speaks directly to her Beloved: "O my God!"; and then, "heavenly Father" and again with Christ who is Love crucified.

Teresa tells Christ the story of her own love, in three movements. In the first, *as happens in human love, the one who loves desires solitude and exclusiveness. "Only you." "Alone with the One who is Alone" (with the Absolute). "To live as though only God and the soul that loves him exists in the world," was one of her strong experiences.*

In the early steps of her spiritual journey, Teresa, who was a nun in a monastery of 180 religious, senses a call to the desert, accompanied by the temptation to flee: to go far away, where no one would know her name, her face, or her past. Not even later, in the oasis of a totally cloistered life in the Carmels, will she be able to enjoy absolute solitude with the exception of only brief periods. However, the greatest obstacle is an interior one: the nature of love does not allow one to enjoy its delight alone. Love carries another demand.

In the second *movement of her soliloquy: there needs to be other lovers. "O powerful love of God," how you are different from worldly love. "Your love seeks nothing but company." The more lovers you have, the more you grow in love. This is her experience. On one occasion she happened to enjoy a not so frequent solitude in the castle of her soul. Here she found the space for absolute intimacy with God. However, as she is about to reach the most secret and profound room of the castle, an irresistible force draws her to the gate and its surroundings to shout out to the world. She says, "The soul would want to be living right in the midst of the world so as to influence even one more soul to praise God more. A woman in this state of soul becomes afflicted by the hindrance caused by her nature . . . and she*

*is jealous of those who have the freedom to cry out and make known
in public who this great God of hosts is" (*Castle *VI:6, 3).
The* third *movement: to love with Christ. "O my Jesus, how great is
your love for all people." "We see how you demonstrated this by
shedding so much blood." [To love] with God who shapes within us
true love. "Whoever fails to love one's neighbor, fails to love You,
my Lord."
In her prayer, founded in love, Teresa arrives at the great discovery:
whoever loves God is irresistibly led to love one's neighbors.*

1. I often reflect, my Lord, that if there is something by which life
can endure being separated from You, it is solitude. For the soul rests
in the quiet of solitude; yet, since it is not completely free for the
enjoyment of solitude, the torment is often doubled. But the torment
arising from the obligation to deal with creatures and from not being
allowed to be alone with one's Creator makes the soul consider that
first torment a delight. But why is this, my God, that quiet tires the
soul that aims only at pleasing You? Oh, powerful love of God, how
different are your effects from those of the world's love! This latter
love doesn't want company since company would seem to oblige it to
give what it possesses. In the case of the love of my God, the more
lovers that love knows there are, the more it increases; and so its joys
are tempered by seeing that not all enjoy that good. O my God, what
is this that happens: in the greatest favors and consolations coming
from You, the memory grieves over the many there are who don't want
these consolations and over those who will lose them forever! So the
soul looks for ways to find company, and willingly sets aside its joy
when it thinks it can be of some help that others might strive to enjoy
it.

2. But, my heavenly Father, wouldn't it be more worthwhile to leave
aside these desires until a time when the soul has less experience of
Your favors, and now be completely occupied in enjoying You? Oh,
my Jesus, how great is the love You bear the children of men, for the
greatest service one can render You is to leave You for their sake and
their benefit — and then You are possessed more completely. For
although the will isn't so satisfied through enjoyment, the soul rejoices
because it is pleasing You. And it sees that while we live this mortal
life, earthly joys are uncertain, even when they seem to be given by
You, if they are not accompanied by love of neighbor. Whoever fails
to love his neighbor, fails to love You, my Lord, since we see You
showed the very great love You have for the children of Adam by
shedding so much blood.

94.
THIRD SOLILOQUY
A GREAT AFFLICTION HAS TAKEN HOLD OF MY SOUL

This may seem unusual to us. A mystic, captured by love, plunges into a meditation on sin. Likewise, Saint Paul, through the mystery of Christ, discovers the mystery of iniquity. Saint Teresa does not fall into a mere meditative or intellectual contemplation. In the face of the reality of sin, she feels moved to consider her own personal involvement and to being its accomplice in a way no one else can be. She never lost the concrete sense of evil that plays its role in life. She feels like a "sinner," and places herself amongst the "sinners" referred to in the Scriptures, from David to the Samaritan woman, to Peter and Paul; these are her saints, the ones who have experienced the bitterness of sin, even though none of them — she retains — has been as determined as her to resist God. While writing The Interior Castle, *in a moment when her spiritual life is approaching its culmination, she dedicates one of its chapters to how the awareness of the nature of sin resurfaces in the Christian who reaches the fullness of grace and love: in the form of a dense and penetrating suffering, void of anxiety or fear of hell; as a thorn that stimulates love and purifies it.*

In the following soliloquy, the meditation on sin begins with love: in the beginning there was love. A love that prepared the way for glory, the sorrowful love of the Son, a lesson in love that teaches us how to love. Then she introduces the drama of sin and the pain it causes her to reflect upon it. "A great affliction takes hold of my soul" (as in Gethsemane: "My soul is sad, even unto death").

During the remainder of the meditation her sentiments center on a personal reflection.

Sin is of interest to her more as a fact of love and the absence of love than as a mystery full of its own considerations. To sin is to forget: to cancel out any recall of the goodness that surrounds and clothes us; to become oblivious to our true selves and to our values. The person who sins finds oneself without memory. Evil traumatizes a person's capacity to recall the primordial elements of one's life. This forgetfulness becomes ingratitude. And "how the greatness of Your favor, Lord, harms those who are ungrateful!" as though the gift received would determine the measure of one's emptiness.

Here the meditation takes a turn toward petition and praise: "My soul, bless forever a God so great!" "Blessed be such a Lord, blessed such boundless mercy." The psalm that protests the hardness of the heart comes to her lips: "How long will your hearts be hardened?" And then she points to the figure of Christ who is "meek and just." The mystery of sin, however, bears a luminous tract: the Father's forgiveness. God lifts back up the one who falls, he never ceases to welcome the one who loves him, and forever responds to the one who calls. The person who comes back from sin immediately finds two inseparable companions – memory and love. Encouraged by memory and impelled by love the soul will live on by means of this dual guide, sweetened by the concrete presence of Christ. "You have cured my blindness with the blindfold that covered Your divine eyes and my vanity with that cruel crown of thorns!"

After this alternating back and forth of the memory and love, the "only cure" comes into relief – as an opening to life – the pure desire to see God, so as to free oneself forever from evil: "I don't know if this weariness will be taken away until all the miseries of this mortal life are removed by seeing You."

This stream of sentiments that flows through this meditation takes its force from a particular Christian perspective of sin: sin is, above all, something meaningless, similar to a moment of rage that interrupts the course of life (and Teresa petitions): "Come back and give us a hand, and awaken us from such an incurable rage so as to incite us to ask you for your healing." But in an even more profound manner, sin is a human factor capable of drawing God and Christ into our condition of being poor creatures who possess, however, a divine calling.

1. My soul grew greatly distressed, my God, while considering the glory You've prepared for those who persevere in doing Your will, the number of trials and sufferings by which Your Son gained it, and how much love in its greatness, which at such a cost taught us to love, deserves our gratitude. How is it possible, Lord, that all this love is forgotten and that mortals are so forgetful of You when they offend You? O my Redeemer, and how completely forgetful of themselves they are! What great goodness is Yours, that You then remember us, and that though we have fallen through the moral wound we inflicted on You, You return to us, forgetful of this, to lend a hand and awaken us from so incurable a madness, that we might seek and beg salvation of you! Blessed be such a Lord; blessed be such great mercy; and praised forever such tender compassion!

2. Oh, my soul, bless forever so great a God. How is it possible to turn against Him? Oh, how the greatness of Your favor, Lord, harms those who are ungrateful! May You, my God, provide the remedy. Children of men, how long will you be hard of heart and keep your hearts opposed to this most meek Jesus? What is this? Shall our wickedness against Him perhaps endure? No, for the life of man comes to an end like the flower of the field, and the Virgin's Son must come to give that terrible sentence. O my powerful God! Since even though

we may not so desire, You must judge us, why don't we consider how important it is to please You before that hour comes? But who, who will not want so just a Judge? Blessed will they be who in that fearful moment rejoice with You, my God and Lord! The soul You have raised up has known how miserably lost it was for the sake of gaining a very brief satisfaction, and it is determined to please You always. Since You, my soul's Good, do not fail those who desire You or cease to respond to those who call upon You, what remedy, through Your favor, Lord, will You provide that the soul may be able to live afterward and not be dying over the remembrance of having lost the great good it once possessed through the innocence that came from baptism? The best life it can have is to die always with this feeling of compunction. But the soul that loves You tenderly, how can it bear this?

3. Yet, what foolishness I'm asking You, my Lord! It seems I've forgotten Your grandeurs and mercies and how You've come into the world of sinners and have purchased us for so great a price and have paid for our false joys by suffering such cruel torments and blows. You have cured my blindness with the blindfold that covered Your divine eyes and my vanity with that cruel crown of thorns!

O Lord, Lord! All this saddens more the one who loves You. The only consolation is that Your mercy will be praised forever when my wickedness is known. Nevertheless, I don't know if this weariness will be taken away until all the miseries of this mortal life are removed by seeing You.

95.
FOURTH SOLILOQUY
GIVE ME BACK, LORD, THE TIME THAT I LOST

"To see you," was the final cry of the preceding soliloquy. The following one is marked by the phrase "to consider the joy of being with you."

The seventeen soliloquies were written in an intense atmosphere of eschatological hope which for years has kept the Author in continuous expectation of the imminent encounter with the Lord, living against the clock: "It doesn't appear to me that there is anything to live for but this. . . . When I hear the clock sound it makes me joyful because I realize that another hour of life has past and I am closer to the moment of seeing God" (Life, *40:20*).

In The Interior Castle, *the last chapter of the sixth dwelling place speaks of "desires of enjoying the presence of God so strong and impetuous as to put one's life in danger."*

Just the same, whether they be strong desires to see God or the peaceful nostalgia for heaven, which opens the following soliloquy, they both prove powerless in uprooting the earthly life. This is not the course her soliloquy takes. Instead, as if by reflex, they unleash the desire to consume this life "in service." Her prayer turns toward service, moved also by an immense nostalgia for the time she wasted. "How late have my desires been enkindled and how early, Lord, were you seeking and calling that I might be totally taken up with you!" It is Augustine's cry that echoes: "So late have I come to know you, O Beauty. . . ."

This sentiment directed toward her past life, and in part poorly made use of, pervades throughout the whole meditation. How can one make up for such a loss? Life is irreversible, yet it still must be recuperated. It must be redeemed in order to render to God the existence it has received.

Teresa turns to Him, not to present to him such a stimulating concern, but to draw near to "his sovereign power." "If you are so powerful, so omnipotent, as in fact you are, what can be impossible to you?" "I firmly believe that you can do whatever you want."

Her prayer progresses in pure petition, incited by this sense of lost time, as though there were an emptiness that needed to be filled. She doesn't digress into suggesting possible solutions: for example, to lengthen, even painfully, the years of her life so as to compensate the voids of the past; or even to make up for lost time by increasing the present intensity of her life. No. Teresa places herself back into God: "You know very well, my God, that in the midst of all my miseries I never failed to acknowledge Your great power and mercy."

The entire soliloquy centers on a single request: "Recover, my God, the time that I lost." It is a petition she repeats without any traces of self-centeredness. Her prayer does not call to mind the parable of the talents, but the prayer of the leper: "If you want it, you can do it . . ." and the desire for the bridal gown in order to appear before the King.

1. It seems, my Lord, my soul finds rest in considering the joy it will have if through Your mercy the fruition of Yourself is granted it. But first it would want to serve You since it will be enjoying what You, in serving it, have gained for it. What shall I do, my Lord? What shall I do, my God? Oh, how late have my desires been enkindled and how early, Lord, were You seeking and calling that I might be totally taken up with You! Do You perhaps, Lord, abandon the wretched or withdraw from the poor beggar when he wants to come to You? Do Your grandeurs or Your magnificent works, Lord, perhaps have a limit? O my God and my Mercy, how You can show them now in Your servant! You are mighty, great God! Now it can be known whether my soul understands itself in being aware of the time it has lost and of how in a moment You, Lord, can win this time back again. It seems foolish to me, since they usually say lost time cannot be recovered. May You be blessed, my God!

2. O Lord, I confess Your great power. If You are powerful, as You are, what is impossible for You who can do everything? Please my Lord, give the order, give the order, for although I am miserable, I firmly believe You can do what You desire. And the more I hear of Your greater marvels and consider that You can add to them, the more my faith is strengthened; and I believe with greater determination that You will do this. What is there to marvel at in what the Almighty does? You know well, my God, that in the midst of all my miseries I never failed to acknowledge Your great power and mercy. May that in which I have not offended You, Lord, help me.

Recover, my God, the lost time by giving me grace in the present and future so that I may appear before You with wedding garments; for if You want to, You can do so.

96.
FIFTH SOLILOQUY
PRAYER OF PETITION. IT IS ALSO LOVE TO ASK

This time Teresa wants to present a request to the Lord. But she will succeed to do so only at the end. Almost the entire soliloquy is spent on a concern that impedes her way and which she explains at great length to God.

She is perplexed by this question: Should a person like herself dare to ask something from God, or should she keep silent? How can someone who has been so negligent in guarding what has been given to her, dare ask for something else? And how can someone remain silent, when the Lord himself, the One who knows all things, tells us to ask because he will not refrain from giving?

For Teresa, this is not a theological or theoretical concern. Nor is it mere protocol that prepares the way for her request. It is her way of life. It is a perennial question. Oftentimes, in the moment of "receiving," she had adopted the gesture to stop the giving hands of God to tell him that he should be careful of what he is doing, that he should not place his gifts in the hands of someone so ungrateful, nor should he pour his precious liqueur in a vessel so broken (cf. Life, 18:4).

On the other hand, she revives through her own profound experience the evangelical invitation to ask and whose promise assures that the request will be heard: "He promised me that whatever I would have asked him, He would have never denied it to me, knowing fully well I never would have asked him for something contrary to his glory" (Life, 39:1).

Martha and the event at Bethany offer Teresa the solution to her concern. "That holy woman by the name of Martha," when presenting her complaint to Christ, does not ask for less toil in her service, but for greater love. Love also means to ask God for something. "Love gives equal value to all things." "The one thing necessary" is that love be not impeded to love. The prayer proceeds from Martha's complaint to Teresa's petition. "How can I love you, my God, as you ought to be loved, if you do not unite my love to the love you give to me?"

The love that He has for the one who prays makes it impossible for Teresa to utter Martha's complaint. Teresa had the same fate as Mary: "I always found in my God manifestations of his love that were far greater than the ones I ever managed to ask for or desire."

The moment to which the soliloquy was leading has now arrived. Teresa, in formulating her petition, makes three specific requests:

— grant me, O God, something that I can give to you (like Saint Augustine);

— remember that I am a creature molded by you (like the psalmist: "do not despise the work of you own hands");
— let me know who my Creator is so that I might find a way to love him. In these three requests Teresa joins the spirit of Saint Augustine with the voice of the psalmists. Otherwise, "What could a creature so wretched as myself ever ask for?"

1. O my Lord, how does anyone who has so poorly served You and so poorly known how to keep what You have given her dare ask for favors? What can be entrusted to one who has often been a traitor? What, then, shall I do, Consoler of the disconsolate and Cure for anyone who wants to be cured by You? Would it be better, perhaps, to keep still about my needs, hoping You will provide the remedy for them? Certainly not; for You, my Lord and my delight, knowing the many needs there must be and the comfort it is for us to rely on You, tell us to ask you and that You will not fail to give.

2. I sometimes remember the complaint of that holy woman, Martha. She did not complain only about her sister, rather, I hold it is certain that her greatest sorrow was that the thought that You, Lord, did not feel sad about the trial she was undergoing and didn't have as much love for her as for her sister. This must have caused her greater sorrow than did serving the one for whom she had such great love; for love turns work into rest. It seems that in saying nothing to her sister but in directing her whole complaint to You, Lord, that love made her dare to ask why You weren't concerned. And even Your reply seems to refer to her complaints as I have interpreted it, for love alone is what gives value to all things; and a kind of love so great that nothing hinders it is the one thing necessary. But how can we possess, my God, a love in conformity with what the Beloved deserves, if Your love does not join love with itself? Shall I complain with this holy woman? Oh, I have no reason at all, for I have always seen in my God much greater and more extraordinary signs of love than I have known how to ask for or desire! If I don't complain about the many things Your kindness has suffered for me, I have nothing to complain about. What, then, can so miserable a thing as I ask for? That You, my God, give to me what I might give to You, as St. Augustine says, so that I may repay You something of the great debt I owe You; that You remember that I am the work of Your hands; and that I may know who my Creator is in order to love Him.

97.
SIXTH SOLILOQUY
FOR HOW LONG WILL I BE COMPELLED TO WAIT

The outline of the sixth soliloquy is not as uniform. It begins immediately with a loud cry. The cry reaches its height with a sorrowful lament. Finally, the tone drops returning to a serene and meditative soliloquy: a self-invitation to wait, in calm and without restriction.

The reader who adheres to Teresa's prayer is taken back by the impact of the initial cry: "How long . . ." "O long life. . ." "O death, death, I don't know who fears you." It's certainly not easy for the reader to perceive the meaning behind this series of interjections. To understand these words one would have to draw nearer to their writer, to see her facial expressions, to know her turmoil, to know the story of her life.

Here, the person who cries from the depths of this soliloquy is going through something tremendous and inexpressible. She tells us this herself in The Story of Her Life *(chapter 20, n. 10-11). With a sudden reference to the horizons of the "next life," she drastically changes attitude about the present life. The ropes that kept her bound to the edge of the earth have loosened. Her life itself with its tone and pace have a different set of dimensions: life is now either too long, or it is short, toilsome, and not fully lived; its course receives the warning of its direction in a new and paradoxical manner; it possesses the desolation of a desert and the confinement of a prison; she perceives it in a different manner both in what passes through her soul, and what effects her bodily.*

Here is where the violent desire emerges and bursts into invocations directed one after the other to God, to life and to death, as if these last two were also responsible persons with whom she could carry on a dialogue. She scolds life for its length; she launches a challenge at death, because it has not yet begun to act. Mystical experience borders on poetry. This reality had already been poetically described by the Author. Here are some of the verses she wrote out against life and against death.

> *"How ever long my anxious life*
> *is kept in exile!"*
> *"How ever tight its bonds*
> *that by now have worn me down!"*

Against death:

> *"Well then, death, make haste*
> *let your golden arrow fly . . . !*
> *I am dying because I am not dying!"*

Also Saint John of the Cross wrote verses that speak of life and death in a similar way.

Just the same, it would be difficult for the reader to grasp what Teresa says in these lyrics, if at first one has not loosened certain ropes that tie one down to this present life alone, or if one hasn't come close to the soul of the Author. To read this prayer is to allow it to penetrate and envelope us.

1. O my delight, Lord of all created things and my God! How long must I wait to see You? What remedy do You provide for one who finds so little on earth that might give some rest apart from You? O long life! O painful life! O life that is not lived! Oh, what lonely solitude; how incurable! Well, when, Lord, when? How long? What shall I do, my God, what shall I do? Should I, perhaps, desire not to desire You? Oh, my God and my Creator, You wound and You do not supply the medicine; You wound and the sore is not seen; You kill, leaving one with more life! In sum, my Lord, being powerful You do what You will. Well, my God, do You want so despicable a worm to suffer these contradictions? Let it be so, my God, since You desire it, for I desire nothing but to love You.

2. But, alas, alas, my Creator, what great pain it causes to complain and speak of what has no remedy until You give one! And the soul so imprisoned wants its freedom, while desiring not to depart one iota from what You want. Desire, my Glory, that its pain increase; or cure it completely. O death, death, I don't know who fears you, since life lies in you! But who will not fear after having wasted a part of life in not loving God? And since I am one of these, what do I ask for and what do I desire? Perhaps the punishment so well deserved for my faults? Don't permit it, my Good, for my ransom cost You a great deal.

3. Oh, my soul! Let the will of God be done; this suits you. Serve and hope in His mercy, for He will cure your grief when penance for your faults will have gained some pardon for them. Don't desire joy but suffering. O true Lord and my King! I'm still not ready for suffering if Your sovereign hand and greatness do not favor me, but with these I shall be able to do all things.

98.
SEVENTH SOLILOQUY
MY SOUL PRAISES THE LORD

*This soliloquy begins with a biblical assertion: "You delight O Lord to dwell with the hearts of men." It is a phrase attributed to divine Wisdom and is found in the Book of Proverbs. Teresa heard and recited these words many times during liturgical prayer. This gallantry of God first discovered in the Liturgy of Hours finds its way into Teresa's own interior liturgy. She listened to these words from deep within, and repeated them, for herself and for the small group of twelve gathered at Saint Joseph's. Each time she calls to mind this biblical text, it produces in her a sense of awe before this incredible gesture of God who transports his heaven into the hearts of human persons: "What is this? When I hear these words, I always experience such great comfort. And I experienced this even at the times I was wanton and reckless. Can it be ever possible, Lord, that a soul which has reached the point of receiving such favors and graces from You, having understood that you delight in her, still fall back and offend you, after being showered with so many of your gifts and proofs of your love?" (*Life, 14:10*).*

Through this biblical verse, the soliloquy begins an elevation of the mystery of love, whose origins lie in the Holy Trinity and whose highest expression lies in the soul of Christ. The love of God in Teresa's soul shifts back and forth between these two poles that are Trinitarian and Christological. There are three basic movements in this prayer.

1 — The initial impact of this biblical passage in Teresa's soul is almost baffling. Having once again understood by way of this biblical assertion that God takes delight in her, Teresa quickly passes from a state of joy to one of awe.

"My soul is enraptured with joy," but then, "what words are these!" In a way similar to what happened to Moses on Mount Sinai, God's closeness makes her perceive the littleness of her own self to the point that she uses the image of a worm when referring to herself.

And as on other occasions, her delicate feminine sensitivity brings her to evoke the worm's "foul odor" before the Lord. It is the inevitable memory of sin in a moment of love.

A question arises out of the depths of her awe: "Is it possible, Lord, that you have no other creatures to take delight in that you need to look to me?" In answer to her question, she shifts spontaneously from the text from Wisdom to a passage of the gospel: "The voice that was heard at the moment of your baptism tells that you find your delight in your Son." Then her soliloquy, like an arrow, shoots out at God with a final question: "Could it be ever possible that we and Christ find each other on the same plane of your love and your delight?"

2 — The question remains unanswered. The soliloquy breaks out into still another advancement toward the depth of this mystery. In the womb of the Trinity there exists boundless delight, an ineffable wave of love in eternal ebb and flow.
Therefore she writes: "Why then do you need my love? Why do you desire it so much, my God? What do you gain from it?"
This new question that arises from Teresa's soul is aimed directly at the persons of the Holy Trinity. It is not the first time that she formulates a question of that kind. Among Teresa's "intimate writings," there is one very brief text (Testimonies, 52), that synthesizes the entire episode, both question and answer, in just a few lines. It speaks on the same topic, with slight variation: "At one time I wanted to do something in service of Our Lord. But I thought upon the little that I could do, and said within myself, 'Why, Lord, do you want my works?' He answered: 'in order to see your will, daughter.' " In this soliloquy, her question does not expect an answer. It concludes on its own with a flow of praise: "May you be forever blessed, My God! May all things praise you without end."

3 — Among all things, however, there is one, whose voice transcends the powerful chorus of all creation: Christ. Outside of the Trinity, within the realm of creation, alongside of us, there truly lives one who loves, praises, and adores God as He merits. In Christ, my own voice of praise and boldness of love acquire meaning. "Rejoice, my soul . . . rejoice." This is how the Author of the Magnificat in being his mother praised and loved God. In the same way, without realizing it, Teresa, in her soliloquy, makes the words of Mary her own as she says in truth: "My soul praises and magnifies the Lord."
This soliloquy traces the itinerary of the praise elevated by the soul to God, from the womb of the Trinity to Christ; from Christ to Mary and to us.

1. O my Hope, my Father, my Creator, and my true Lord and Brother! When I consider how You say that Your delights are with the children of men, my soul rejoices greatly. O Lord of heaven and earth, what words these are that no sinner might be wanting in trust! Are You, Lord, perhaps lacking someone with whom to delight that You seek such a foul-smelling little worm like myself? That voice that was heard at the Baptism says You delight in Your Son. Well, will we all be equal, Lord? Oh, what extraordinary mercy and what favor so beyond our ability to deserve! And that mortals forget all of this! Be

mindful, my God, of so much misery, and behold our weakness, since You are the Knower of everything.

2. O my soul: Consider the great delight and great love the Father has in knowing His Son and the Son in knowing His Father; and the enkindling love with which the Holy Spirit is joined with them; and how no one of them is able to be separated from this love and knowledge, because they are one. These sovereign Persons know each other, love each other, and delight in each other. Well, what need is there for my love? Why do You want it, my God, or what do You gain? Oh, may You be blessed! May You be blessed, my God, forever! May all things praise You, Lord, without end since in You there can be no end.

3. Be joyful, my soul, for there is someone who loves your God as He deserves. Be joyful, for there is someone who knows His goodness and value. Give thanks to Him, for He has given us on earth someone who thus knows Him, as His only Son. Under this protection you can approach and petition Him, for then His Majesty takes delight in you. Don't let any earthly thing be enough to separate you from your delight, and rejoice in the grandeur of God; in how He deserves to be loved and praised; that He helps you to play some small role in the blessing of His name; and that you can truthfully say: My soul magnifies and praises the Lord.

99.
EIGHTH SOLILOQUY
YOU HAVE WORDS OF LIFE

*Prayer is a conversation between friends. In the book of her spiritual experiences (*Life, *8:5), Saint Teresa had written that it is a "question of friendship." This conversation is comprised of two segments: a listening and a reply. The word from the Other can reach my ear through a way that is entirely interior and silent. Ordinarily, however, it comes to us from the Bible. At this point my interior silence is broken because His word seeks my reply.*

The present soliloquy allows us to take a surprise look at Saint Teresa as she is living out this conversation. The dialogue takes place three times, maintaining the same inflection and cadence, almost like an outline printed in a manual.

Here, therefore, is the order in which these two segments of the three dialogues appear.

The first *segment (listening): Teresa refers to a passage of the gospel: You possess the words of eternal life, Peter tells you (n. 1); You yourself had said: "Come to me, all" (n. 2); You said, moreover, that you came to save sinners (n. 3).*

In the second *segment, we have her replies, that are both simple and animated. One of them takes on the form of praise. "You are almighty; your works are incomprehensible" (n. 1). The remaining two are in the form of a petition: "Have mercy, Creator, on these your creatures" (n. 2); "Behold, Lord, we are your handiwork. May your goodness and mercy help us" (n. 3).*

There is no place in this conversation for subtleties, plays on words, or for concepts. The old motifs resurface out of the depths of the soul, as fragments of life. After years of reading books whose words were dead, Teresa one day realized that the words of the Bible vibrated with life. One brief phrase, or even just one word can be enough to communicate its life. "I am," "peace be with you," "I will remain with you always . . ." are all words that the Risen Lord returns and says for her. And for anyone who receives them in the heart.

*The greatest absurdity consists in the fact "that we forget your words." Teresa took hold of this paradox at its roots: "All the damage that happens to the world goes back to the sad fact that the truths of the Scriptures are not known in their clarity" (*Life, *40:1).*

Now her reply becomes a moment of contemplation. The word of God, who created the universe, and who could create much more, brings

Saint Teresa before the mystery of God: "O my God, author of all creation . . ." introducing her into the boundless realm of his omnipotence: "You are almighty." This is an attribute of God's that she has celebrated oftentimes through an exquisite interior prayer: "You are a King of infinite sovereignty, my God, because the reign you possess, you have not leased, it belongs to you. When in the Creed we recite: 'your kingdom will have no end' I feel as though this affirmation were a special gift. I praise you and I bless you, Lord, because of the certainty that your reign will last forever" (Way, 22:1).

Teresa's Creed is at once a profession of faith and a hymn of praise. Her prayer then becomes a supplication: "Bring it about, then, Lord, that my thoughts not withdraw from Your words."

As the prayer proceeds, the soliloquy produces a peculiar effect on the reader. Teresa's personal experience has a definite focus. Her prayer is a meeting and a conversation with God. She had always insisted on the character of "solitude": to pray is to be "alone" before God, as Moses, who stood before the burning bush in the middle of the desert. Immediacy, solitude, and intimacy may appear to be the principal elements of this conversation that guard it against any outside interference.

But instead the opposite occurs. As her prayer unfolds, the soliloquy assumes a tone of calling out to others. The reader feels oneself joined to the Author, a participant in her supplication. From the singular, her words quickly shift to the plural. Both writer and reader find themselves gathered together in the word of Christ: "Come to me, all." Just as in the Our Father. We find ourselves closely united together in both need and supplication, overflowing in the same sentiments and verbal expression. When rereading it, it is fascinating to note its effectiveness. The Author suddenly identifies herself with all her readers, with the blind person in the gospel. "Have mercy, Creator, on these your creatures! Behold, we don't understand or know what we desire. . . . Lord, give us light; behold, the need is greater than with the man born blind. . . ."

Then once again, the prayer returns to an incandescent composition of supplication and praise. "Let your mercy shine . . . ; behold, Lord, we are your handiwork. May your goodness and mercy help us."

1. O Lord, my God, how You possess the words of eternal life, where all mortals will find what they desire if they want to seek it! But what a strange thing, my God, that we forget Your words in the madness and sickness our evil deeds cause! O my God, God, God, author of all creation! And what is creation if You, Lord, should desire to create more? You are almighty; Your works are incomprehensible. Bring it about, then, Lord, that my thoughts not withdraw from Your words.

2. You say: Come to me all who labor and are burdened, for I will comfort you. What more do we want, Lord? What are we asking for? What do we seek? Why are those in the world so unhappy if not because of seeking rest? God help me! Oh, God help me! What is this Lord? Oh, what a pity! Oh, what great blindness, that we seek rest where it is impossible to find it! Have mercy, Creator, on these Your creatures. Behold, we don't understand or know what we desire, nor do we obtain what we ask for. Lord, give us light; behold, the need is greater than with the man born blind, for he wanted to see the light and couldn't. Now, Lord, there is no desire to see. Oh, how incurable an illness! Here, my God, is where Your power must be demonstrated; here, Your mercy.

Oh, what a difficult thing I ask You, my true God: that You love someone who doesn't love You, that You open to one who doesn't knock, that You give health to one who likes to be sick and goes about looking for sickness. You say, My Lord, that You come to seek sinners; these, Lord, are real sinners. Don't look at our blindness, my God, but at all the blood Your Son shed for us. Let Your mercy shine upon evil that has so increased; behold, Lord, we are Your handiwork. May Your goodness and mercy help us.

100.
NINTH SOLILOQUY
O LIVING FOUNT OF MY GOD

There are two passages in St. John's Gospel that always produce a strong impression on Saint Teresa. The one in which Jesus offers living water to the Samaritan woman at the well of Jacob (Jn 4:10-14), and the episode at the temple during the Feast of Tabernacles: "On the last and greatest day of the festival Jesus stood up and cried out, 'If anyone thirsts, let him come to me; let him drink who believes in me. Scripture has it: "from within him rivers of living water shall flow " ' " (Jn 7:37-38).

This evangelical invitation and the image of the living water ignite an ardent thirst in Teresa. Already in her book The Way of Perfection *she had revealed this same desire, though remaining anonymous:*

"O my Lord! What keeps me from being so immersed in this living water to the point that it causes me to die? Could it be impossible for this to happen? No, for the love and desire for God can grow to such a point that it can take us over the brim. . . . I know a person whose thirst was so ardent that she could clearly see that it was bringing her close to death, should the Lord have not come to give her this living water in such great abundance for she was almost carried completely outside of herself with raptures" (n. 8).

So too, in this present soliloquy, the evangelical passage that invites all to drink of Christ opens the way for her to this fount of new desires, which she transforms into prayer: prayer that asks for living water. However, this biblical text imposes on Teresa's prayer an unexpected variation. It is already evident that she burns with thirst. Just the same, the invitation of Jesus is also universal: "Come to me, all." All — even those who are burning in the living flames of earthly greed. They too are in "great need of water," so as not to be totally consumed. Teresa's prayer goes out to them and becomes a supplication formulated with great boldness for their sake. It is not enough that Christ invite them to come, for they may be unable to or simply don't wish to do so: "Come to them Yourself, my God." Certainly, once they have tasted this water, they will come to life again.

After speaking on behalf of the others, it is now her turn: "O Life, who gives life to all! Do not deny me this sweetest water." And since the Lord has promised it to "those who want it," she draws near to him with a very large jar: "I want it, Lord, and I beg for it, and I come to You." The crescendo of this three-part statement (I desire it, I beg for it, I come to You) is her personal response to the universal invitation: "Come to me, all." After a brief moment of prayer, Teresa moves from desire to fulfillment, as though she had with her own lips

touched the living fount of the Savior: "O living founts from the
wounds of my God, how you have flowed with great abundance for
our sustenance."
The soliloquy culminates in this sense of full satisfaction and con-
templation: the living water that flows without end, "always," "with
great abundance," sustaining us in the elation of this "divine liqueur."

1. O compassionate and loving Lord of my soul! You likewise say: Come to me all who thirst, for I will give you drink. How can anyone who is burning in the living flames of cupidity for these miserable earthly things fail to experience great thirst? There is an extraordinary need for water so that one might not be completely consumed by this fire. I already know, my Lord, that out of Your goodness You will give it. You Yourself say so; Your words cannot fail. Well, if those accustomed to living in this fire and to being reared in it, no longer feel it or, like fools, do not succeed in recognizing their great need, what remedy is there, my God? You've come into the world as a remedy for needs such as these. Begin, Lord! Your compassion must be shown in the most difficult situations. Behold, my God, Your enemies are gaining a great deal. Have pity on those who have no pity on themselves; now that their misfortune has placed them in a state in which they don't want to come to You, come to them Yourself, my God. I beg this of You in their name; and I know that as they understand and turn within themselves and begin to taste You, these dead ones will rise.

2. O Life, who gives life to all! Do not deny me this sweetest water that You promise to those who want it. I want it, Lord, and I beg for it, and I come to You. Don't hide Yourself, Lord, from me, since You know my need and that this water is the true medicine for a soul wounded with love of You. O Lord, how many kinds of fire there are in this life! Oh, how true it is that one should live in fear! Some kinds of fire consume the soul, other kinds purify it that it might live ever rejoicing in You. O living founts from the wounds of my God, how you have flowed with great abundance for our sustenance, and how surely he who strives to sustain himself with this divine liqueur will advance in the midst of the dangers of this life.

101.
TENTH SOLILOQUY
LORD, RAISE THESE DEAD

This meditation centers on the mystery of sin and is divided into three parts: 1) Christ is reached through the sin of mankind; 2) we are all sinners, full of faults; 3) prayer of reconciliation with Christ before the mystery of the iniquity present in human history.

1 — *Even the sins of mankind revolve around Christ, the only center of all things, as a generator of both evil and grace: "How we hasten to offend You!" God, however, hastens with even greater effort to pardon us.*
The prayer of Teresa's soul becomes a dialogue that asks a question of Christ himself: Why? "What reason is there, Lord, for such deranged boldness?" Is it because of the certainty of your mercy? The reply comes from an unexpected biblical passage: "Deadly enemies surround me" (Ps 17:5), which causes Teresa to react with this incisive statement: "What a serious thing sin is, for it was enough to kill God!"

2 — *Her dialogue shifts now from Christ to her fellow human beings: "O Christians, it's time to defend your King!" Sin is not child's play, nor an accepted phantom, and not even an error of vast human proportion. Instead, it is a tragedy, whose principal actors are both the human person and God; it is the breakdown of their relationship; it is the choice of being slaves of Lucifer instead of the Lord's. It means being friends on the surface, but traitors deep down, a repetition of the story of Judas and Jesus. Teresa perceives here a more realistic view of the Christian world, which is also filled with excuses, cover-ups, and masks that conceal the evil we commit.*
She hesitates a moment as if to ask herself to whom she should direct her thoughts: "O true friend! . . . O true Christians! . . ." Teresa herself feels overwhelmed by her own awareness of being a poor sinner and sharer in the disease of violence and delinquency of her fellow human beings: "O my God, how You bear in mind the faults I have committed against You!" Her prayer now culminates in supplication for herself and for us: that just one word or tear might give us back our lives, as happened for Lazarus; that the voice of the Lord "be so powerful that even though they do not beg life of You, You give it to them so that afterward, my God, they might come forth from the depth of their own delights."

3 — *Saint Teresa's supplication now dissolves into a gentle prayer. Sin appears as a tomb: whoever sins, enters into the realm of death, as*

Lazarus. Teresa identifies herself with Mary Magdalene: "Lazarus did not ask You to raise him up. You did it for a woman sinner." Well then, "here I am!" "I, although miserable, ask You. . . ." She reaches the point of daring to share with him a personal reflection: "You already know, my King, what torment it is for me to see them so forgetful of the great endless torments they will suffer, if they don't return to You." Teresa's prayer developed an always greater space for others. At the same time, it depicts a God always closer and more good, a "true friend," a God of mercy, besides being Lord, and the sovereign King and judge of all mankind.

1. O God of my soul, how we hasten to offend You and how You hasten even more to pardon us! What reason is there, Lord, for such deranged boldness? Could it be that we have already understood Your great mercy and have forgotten that Your justice is just?

The sorrows of death surround me. Oh, oh, oh, what a serious thing sin is, for it was enough to kill God with so many sorrows! And how surrounded You are by them, my God! Where can You go that they do not torment You? Everywhere mortals wound You.

2. O Christians, it's time to defend your King and to accompany Him in such great solitude. Few are the vassals remaining with Him, and great the multitude accompanying Lucifer. And what's worse is that these latter appear as His friends in public and sell Him in secret. He finds almost no one in whom to trust. O true Friend, how badly he pays You back who betrays You! O true Christians, help your God weep, for those compassionate tears are not only for Lazarus but for those who were not going to want to rise, even though His Majesty call them. O my God, how You bear in mind the faults I have committed against You! May they now come to an end, Lord, may they come to an end, and those of everyone. Raise up these dead; may Your cries be so powerful that even though they do not beg life of You, You give it to them so that afterward, my God, they might come forth from the depth of their own delights.

3. Lazarus did not ask You to raise him up. You did it for a woman sinner; behold one here, my God, and a much greater one; let Your mercy shine. I, although miserable, ask life for those who do not want to ask it of You. You already know, my King, what torment it is for me to see them so forgetful of the great endless torments they will suffer, if they don't return to You.

O you who are accustomed to delights, satisfactions, and consolations, and to always doing your own will, take pity on yourselves! Recall that you will have to be subject forever and ever, without end, to the infernal furies. Behold, behold that the Judge who will condemn you now asks you; and that your lives are not safe for one moment.

Why don't you want to live forever? Oh, hardness of human hearts! May Your boundless compassion, my God, soften these hearts.

102.
ELEVENTH SOLILOQUY
THE MYSTERY OF HELL SEEN THROUGH LOVE

Teresa completes the meditation on sin begun in the previous soliloquy. The most profound aspect inherent in the mystery of sin is hell. Saint Teresa approaches this reality with the eyes of a mystic and as a prophet in prayer.

1 — *At a very precise moment in her mystical journey, Teresa had an experience of the mystery of hell. She gives us an account of it in chapter 32 of* The Book of Her Life: *"I suddenly found that, without knowing how, I had seemingly been put in hell. . . . Were I to live for many years I think it would be impossible for me to forget it"* (Life, *32:1). Because of this experience, the nature of this next soliloquy acquires a backing of personal testimony, convinced as she is that her words in no way express the reality she has seen.*

2 — *A mystic with the soul of a prophet. Shifting her attention away from her personal experience, she energetically addresses her fellow human beings, as would a prophet of the Old Testament. Who could have ever closed our eyes? It is impossible for her not to shout out and denounce this senseless game for which people waste their lives.*

3 — *A mystic with the soul of a prophet in prayer. The act of announcing now turns into prayer. First of all, an invocation directed to God: "O Lord, my God!" Then, an invocation drenched in tears: "I weep for the time I didn't understand," humbly identifying herself with those "whose souls' eyes are covered with mud." At this point of her supplication elevated to God, an unnamed person, though very watchful and present, enters the scene: the Lord grants her a spark of light which she herself will find a way to transmit to others.*
The soliloquy concludes in Christologic fashion. Her petition is not arrogant or founded upon personal motives or merits. "Through the merits of Christ," through his wounds, through the forgiveness with which he pardoned us, "[Father], forgive us."

1. Oh, God help me! Oh, God help me! How great a torment it is for me when I consider what a soul that has always here below been valued, loved, served, esteemed, and pampered will feel when after having died finds itself lost forever, and understands clearly that this loss is endless. (Forgetting about the truths of faith will be no help there, as it is here below.) Also what a torment it is for me to consider what a soul will feel when it finds itself separated from what seemingly

it will not yet have begun to enjoy (and rightly so, for all that which ends with life is but a breath of wind), and surrounded by that deformed and pitiless company with whom it will always have to suffer. It will be placed in that fetid lake filled with snakes, and the bigger the snake, the bigger the bite; in that miserable darkness where it will only see what gives it torment and pain, without seeing any light other than a dark flame! Oh, how ineffective exaggeration is in expressing what this suffering is!

2. O Lord, who placed so much mud in the eyes of this soul that it has not seen these things before it sees them there? O Lord, who stopped its ears that it didn't hear the many times these things were explained to it or of the eternity of these torments? O life that shall not end! O torment without end! O torment without end! How is it they don't fear you, those who are afraid to sleep on a hard bed lest they cause their body discomfort?

3. O Lord, my God! I weep for the time I didn't understand; and since You know, my God, the great number who don't want to understand, I now beg You, Lord, let there be at least one, at least one who will see Your light so that many might possess it. Not through my merits, Lord, for I don't deserve it, but through the merits of Your Son. Behold His wounds, Lord, and since He pardoned those who inflicted them, may You pardon us.

103.
TWELFTH SOLILOQUY
SIN, A MYSTERY OF INIQUITY

Saint Teresa begins on the basis of a biblical text: "My God and my strength" (Ps 42:2), and then continues her thoughts on the mystery of sin. The panorama is obscure and profound, whose dimensions are cosmic and relevant to the universal history of mankind. With this in mind, Teresa's prayer can be divided into two parts: the first, is an invocation to God made in a long and deeply motivated cry (n. 1-3); the second, an appeal to others; a supplication addressed to them, but at the same time made in the presence of God with whom she continues to speak (n. 4-5).

1 — *The mystery of sin is perceived by Teresa as a drama whose setting is human history and whose actors are mankind, God, the devil, Christ. In this effort to penetrate the mystery of sin which influenced the life of mankind, three different perspectives animate the scene.*
Psychological: *sin is an interior tragedy of the human person, which blinds the reason; a radical madness accompanied by that peculiar power of physical strength found in frenzied persons. "Poor and sick are those who withdraw themselves from my God!"*
Theological: *every sin conceals within itself mankind's colossal act of imposing arms against the divinity. She repeats before God the gospel story of the Passion of Christ: He, "bound and tied by the love he bears us" and they "who inflict blows and wounds on him."*
Sociological: *before the spectacle of humanity that tortures itself from generation to generation, tearing itself to pieces due to hatred, war and injustice, she asks herself if truly at the root of human history there isn't a satanic influence. It's as though the mystery of sin couldn't be conceivable without a definite reference to Evil, to the captain of misfortune, yet who is "so poor that he is driven away from the heavenly riches."*
Saint Teresa's prayer in view of the mystery of sin, as on other occasions in view of the "great misfortunes of the Church," is first of all one of supplication: You who are Wisdom, for "all the love you have for creatures," "You who tend to our healing and provide it for us." The soliloquy then becomes a supplication to her fellow human beings: "O mortals, return, return to yourselves!" "understand for love of God," realize that you are living the hour of mercy and "we shall never finish understanding the splendor of our Lord's mercies." May we never lose sight that his justice is just as great as his mercy.

1. O my God and my true Fortitude! What is this, Lord, that we are

cowards about everything except being against You? In opposing You, all the strength of the children of Adam is used up. And if their reason weren't so blind, the reasoning of all together wouldn't suffice for them to dare to take up arms against their Creator, and sustain a continual war against one who in a moment can plunge them into the abyss. But since they are blind, they are like madmen seeking their death because in their imagination it seems to them that by death they gain life. In sum, they are like people without reason. What can we do, my God, with those who have this infirmity of madness? It is said that evil itself brings them great strength. Thus, those who withdraw from my God are sick people because all their fury is turned against You who give them every good.

2. O incomprehensible Wisdom! How necessary is all the love You have for creatures in order to endure so much madness and to wait for our cure and strive to bring it about through a thousand ways and means and remedies! It is something frightening to me when I consider that we lack the strength to be restrained in some very light matter (for they are truly convinced that they are unable to give up an occasion and withdraw from a danger where they may lose their souls), and yet we have strength and courage to attack a Majesty as great as Yours. What is this, my God? What is this? Who gives this strength? Isn't the captain, whom they follow in this battle against You, Your slave damned to eternal fire? Why does one rise up against You? How does the conquered one give courage? How is it they follow one so poor that he is driven away from the heavenly riches? What can anyone give who has nothing himself, other than a lot of unhappiness? What is this, my God? What is this, my Creator? Where does all this strength against You come from, and all this cowardice against the devil? Such an attitude would be the wrong way to attain what You have kept for us eternally and to realize that all the devil's joys and promises are false and traitorous, even if You, my Prince, did not favor Your own, even if we owed something to this prince of darkness. What can we expect from him who was against You?

3. Oh, great blindness, my God! What extraordinary ingratitude, my King! What incurable madness, that we serve the devil with what You, my God, give us! Shall we repay the great love You bear us by loving the one who so abhors You and must abhor You forever? After the blood You shed for us, and the blows and great sorrows You suffered, and the severe torments You endured, do we, as a substitute for avenging Your heavenly Father (since He doesn't want vengeance, and pardons the great disrespect with which His Son was treated), accept as companions and friends those who disrespectfully treated Him? Since we follow their infernal captain, it is clear we shall all be one and live forever in his company, if Your compassion does not provide

a remedy and bring us back to our senses and pardon us for the past.

4. O mortals, return, return to yourselves! Behold your King, for now you will find Him meek; put an end to so much wickedness; turn your fury and your strength against the one who makes war on you and wants to take away your birthright. Turn, turn within yourselves, open your eyes, with loud cries and tears seek light from the one who gave it to the world. Understand for love of God that you with all your strength are about to kill the one who to give you life lost His own. Behold that it is He who defends you from your enemies. And if all this is not enough, let it be enough for you to know that you cannot do anything against His power and that sooner or later you shall have to pay through eternal fire for such great disrespect and boldness. Why is it you see this Majesty bound and tied by the love He bears us? What more did those who delivered Him to death do, but inflict blows and wounds on Him after He was bound?

5. Oh, my God, how much You suffer for one who grieves so little over Your pains! The time will come, Lord, when You will have to make known Your justice and whether it is the equal of Your mercy. Behold, Christians, let us consider it carefully and we shall never finish understanding the splendor of our Lord's mercies and what we owe Him. For if His justice is so great, alas, what will become of those who have deserved that it be carried out and that it shine forth in them?

104.
THIRTEENTH SOLILOQUY
BLESSED ARE YOU, THE CHURCH OF HEAVEN

Let's take a look at a kind of prayer that does not often pass through Teresa's pen. It is an invocation to the saints of heaven.

As it is a normality for Christians, Teresa always turns in prayer to the Father, to Christ and to the Holy Spirit. She does so, by following the impulses that arise from the presence of all Three who dwell within her soul, or through the strength of prayer itself which is an intimate dialogue with one of the three.

It is not that she avoids the saints, for the saints to whom she turns belong to the family of God. However, she does not invoke them individually, or call them by name. Even the names of Mary, Joseph, and Paul, who are so dear to her, are not mentioned. Nor are the names of other personal friends: "the saints who had been sinners," like Jerome, Augustine, Mary Magdalene, and David.

The soliloquy is addressed to the assembly of heaven. We, too, are included in its cry: we, the Church on earth, cry out to the Church in heaven. The four parts composing the soliloquy each begin by summoning the blessed: "O souls that without fear already have fruition of your joy!" (n. 1).

Then she immediately turns to God, the only one who can grant the wisdom "to understand what it is that is given to those who fight valiantly in the dream of this miserable life" (n. 2). However, God, "merciful Father," already gave to us Christ here on earth (n. 3), and it is truly Christ who is the "inestimable treasure" that gives meaning to our dialogue with the blessed: "O blessed souls who with this precious price knew so well how to profit from it . . . tell us!" (n. 4).

All of you who are in heaven, whose joy is guaranteed and without fear, who give praise while no longer suffering, who have entered eternity, anchored forever in the knowledge of the truth, to you do we on earth implore: "Help our misery."

Our misery consists in the fact that we are still prone to Satan; that we yet know how to understand ("obtain for us understanding") that the truths have become foreign to us; that our liking for what is good and of value has gone corrupt; that we have very little recourse "to You, O Lord."

The "we" that Teresa uses includes we who are her readers. This dangerous terrestrial atmosphere also belongs to us. At this point it comes natural to associate ourselves to Teresa's final invocation: "O blessed souls, tell us . . . help us . . . draw water for those here below."

As in other soliloquies, this prayer ends in a synthesis of biblical and liturgical evocations that nourish and sustain it: Heaven is the "in-

heritance of the Father" (1 Pt 1:19), goodness without end. The blessed are already standing at the Font (cf. Rv 7:17). This is why Teresa, in the manner of a prophet of the Old Testament, incites them to draw water joyously from the font (cf. Is 12:3) for the sake of us who "are dying of thirst" as the poor rich man of the gospel parable (cf. Lk 16:24).

1. O souls that without fear already have fruition of your joy and are always absorbed in praises of my God, happy has been your lot! What great reason you have for being ever engaged in these praises. How my soul envies you, for you are already free from the sorrow such terrible offenses committed against my God cause in these unfortunate times, and from the sorrow of seeing so much ingratitude, and seeing that there is no awareness of the multitude of souls carried away by Satan. O blessed heavenly souls! Help our misery and be our intercessors before the divine mercy that we may be given some of your joy and a share in this clear knowledge you possess.

2. Give us understanding, my God, of what it is that is given to those who fight valiantly in the dream of this miserable life. Obtain for us, O loving souls, understanding of the joy it gives you to see the eternal character of your fruition, and how it is so delightful to see certainly that it will have no end. Oh, how unfortunate we are, my Lord! For we believe in everlasting joy and know the truth well; but with so pronounced a habit of failing to reflect on these truths, they have already become so foreign to our souls that these souls neither know about them nor desire to know about them. O selfish people, greedy for your pleasure and delights; not waiting a short time in order to enjoy them in such abundance, not waiting a year, not waiting a day, not waiting an hour—and perhaps it will take no more than a moment—you lose everything, because of the joy of that misery you see present!

3. Oh, oh, oh, how little we trust You, Lord! How much greater the riches and treasures You entrusted to us, since after His thirty-three years of great trials and so unbearable and pitiable a death, You have given us Your Son; and so many years before we were born! Even knowing that we wouldn't repay You, You didn't want to cease trusting us with such an inestimable treasure, so that it wouldn't be your fault, merciful Father, if we fail to acquire what through Him we can obtain from You.

4. O blessed souls who with this precious price knew so well how to profit and buy an inheritance so delightful and permanent, tell us how you gained such an unending good! Help us, since you are so near the fount; draw water for those here below who are perishing of thirst.

105.
FOURTEENTH SOLILOQUY
TO KNOW AND TO LOVE YOU,
AND TO BE JUDGED BY YOU, O LORD

This soliloquy is one full of emotion, enlivened by contrasting sentiments. It concerns the topic of God's justice, which Teresa develops in her own original style. Since the earliest Christian community, the Church has always given special attention to the moment for the divine judgment of the human person. The judge is Christ. The meeting with Him is the parousia: standing before his presence. For each person, arriving at his presence means to arrive at a definitive moment: to allow ourselves to be judged by God.

Teresa, too, gives close attention to this utmost event and has become aware of the importance of being judged by Christ. Also for her, this judgment means a definitive meeting with Him.

What is unique in Teresa's thought revealed in this soliloquy is that the highlight of this judgment is not so much that of being known and judged by Christ, as much as our own arriving to know Him. To seeing Him. Or more precisely, to see his face, his eyes, his glance. Like a prayerful person who stands before the Pantokrator of the Byzantine mosaics.

By the middle of the soliloquy, Teresa creates room, in an open dialogue with Christ, to whisper two personal thoughts to him.

The first *is the joy of seeing his merciful eyes:*

"How pleasing and delightful Your eyes are to the ones who love You; and You, my God, want to look with love! It seems to me that only one such gentle glance towards souls that you possess as Yours is enough reward for many years of service. How hard it is to explain this unless to those who have already understood how gentle the Lord is!" (n. 1).

The second *refers to the fear of beholding his enraged eyes: "You already know, my Lord, that recalling that I might see Your divine face in anger with me on this frightful day of the final judgment caused me greater fear than all the pain and furies of hell shown to me" (n. 2).*

In The Book of Her Life *and in* The Interior Castle, *Teresa had recounted two contrasting experiences. In* The Book of Her Life: *"the vision of Christ left impressed upon me his incomparable beauty, which still today remains vivid in me. . . . I hold, therefore, that it is impossible, unless the Lord in punishing my sins does not permit me to remember it, that something of another nature could occupy my mind with equal obsession and keep me even one instant from recalling this Lord" (*Life, 37:4).

In The Interior Castle, *recalling the words of Jesus, "Out of my sight,*

*you condemned," she writes: "O future daughters [listen to this voice].
In regard to myself, I assure you, though so miserable, the torments
of hell I experienced were nothing compared to the fear I had at the
thought that one day the damned would see enraged the beautiful,
sweet and merciful eyes of the Lord. I don't think my heart could take
it" (Castle, 9:7; cf. Life, 7:7; 38:21; Way, 26 and Life, 13:22).
Teresa would often ask Isabel of Jesus, the novice with the silvery
voice, to sing the verse: "My eyes see You, good and sweet Jesus."
These various sentiments arise from the expression that opens the
soliloquy: "Lord . . . whoever does not know You does not love You."
This develops into a contemplative wave that widens its reach:
"Christians, Christians! Behold the brotherhood you have with this
great God" (n. 2). "Recognize it and don't despise it" (n. 2). "May I
not fail to enjoy peacefully so much beauty" (n. 2).
"Your Father gave You to us, may I not lose, my Lord, so precious
a jewel" (n. 2).
"This compassionate Lord and God of ours . . . desires our friendship:
who will deny it to him?" (n. 3).
"Let's not lose that royal eagle of God's majesty" (n. 4).
This crescendo of sentiments is sustained by two biblical passages:
— "Understand how good is the Lord" (Ps 33:9);
— and the certainty of his forgiveness: "None of the crimes he
committed shall be remembered against him" (Ez 18:22), "whenever
we are sorry for having offended him."*

1. O my Lord and true God! Whoever does not know You does not
love You. What a great truth this is! But, alas, Lord, there are those
who don't want to know You! A dreadful thing is the hour of death.
But, alas, my Creator, how frightful will be the day when Your justice
will have to be exercised! I often consider, my Christ, how pleasing
and delightful Your eyes are to one who loves You; and You, my God,
want to look with love. It seems to me that only one such gentle glance
towards souls that You possess as Yours is enough reward for many
years of service. Oh, God help me, how hard it is to explain this unless
to those who have already understood how gentle the Lord is!

2. Christians, Christians! Behold the brotherhood you have with this
great God; recognize it and don't despise it, for just as this glance is
agreeable to His lovers, it is frightful with a terrifying wrath for His
persecutors. Oh, how we fail to understand that sin is a battle pitched
against God with all our soul's senses and faculties. He who can commit
more sins, invents more treachery against his King. You already know,
my Lord, that recalling that I might see Your divine faced angered
with me on this frightful day of the final judgment caused me greater
fear than all the pain and furies of hell shown to me. I beg You that

Your mercy may protect me from a thing that would be so sad for me, and thus I beg it of You now, Lord. What can happen to me on earth that would resemble this? I want to possess all, my God. May I not fail to enjoy peacefully so much beauty. Your Father gave You to us, may I not lose, my Lord, so precious a jewel. I confess, eternal Father, I have kept it poorly. But there is still a remedy, Lord, there is still a remedy while we live in this exile.

3. O brothers, O brothers and sons of this God! Let us try hard, let us trust hard, for you know that His Majesty says that if we are sorry for having offended Him our faults and evils will not be remembered. Oh, compassion so measureless! What more do we desire? Is there by chance anyone who is not ashamed to ask for so much? Now is the time to take what this compassionate Lord and God of ours gives us. Since He desires our friendship, who will deny it to one who did not refuse to shed all His blood and lose His life for us? Behold that what He asks for is nothing, since giving it is for our own benefit.

4. O Lord, God, help me! Oh, what hardness! Oh, what foolishness and blindness! If when something is lost (a needle or a sparrow hawk that isn't worth anything other than to give a little pleasure upon seeing it fly through the air) we feel sad, why don't we feel sad upon losing this royal eagle of God's majesty and a kingdom of endless enjoyment? What is this? I don't understand it. My God, cure such a great foolishness and blindness.

106.
FIFTEENTH SOLILOQUY
DESIRES, LOVE, AND SERVICE

It would be difficult to penetrate these soliloquies without placing oneself in a similar attitude of prayer and associating one's own personal prayer with that of Teresa's.

This soliloquy, too, is the fruit of a deep religious experience. Teresa is a woman of desires, whose ardent love leads her to concrete works. She lives in the fullest awareness of the mystery of life that passes, yet does not end. It is a life lived between moments of waiting and of service: waiting on building a dialogue with Christ and service of one's neighbors. She finds herself in full accord with two exceptional persons of prayer: Saint Martin (n. 2) and Saint Paul (n. 3).

The soliloquy builds upon three different requests that stem from three particular sentiments of hers that she carried throughout her life and whose persistence remains:

— how long life seems when lived in expectation of one's final encounter with God, especially when lived in uncertainty and without knowing when the hour will come (n. 1);

— how fortunate we are, however, to make use of this time, and create in it space for the highest desires (n. 2);

— and, "now that we must live, may we live for You," given the fact that life is meant to be lived in love and service. Therefore, you, Teresa "wait . . . and watch with care, for everything passes quickly" (n. 3).

These three sentiments have built upon and overlapped each other during the course of Teresa's inner journey, indicating particular chapters in her story of grace:

— One such moment was marked by strong desires, similar to those of Saint Paul, that made her feel desirous of her separation from the body so as to be with Christ: "A very intense, consuming impulse for God," Teresa would say. "I have longings not to live this apparent life any more. I cannot find any remedy for these longings, since the cure for the desire to see God is death; and I cannot take this cure (Testimonies, *1:3).*

— The feast of Saint Martin (November 1572) providentially found her one day to be in tune with the soul and sentiments of this man of God who "knew beforehand the precise day of his death," and who, while seeing it approach, was able to accept its seeming delay "in order to serve his people." Like Saint Martin, Saint Teresa lives the alternative of her serene expectation: she integrates the desires of her final encounter with Christ to her service for others on earth. In this way, she can "have works," and not "only words." When she is unable

to accomplish any works, at least "may my desires be worthwhile, my God."
— Then, as she is immersed in new foundations, trips, and meetings on an ecclesial level where "works" are the sign of orthodoxy, Teresa cannot escape a profound doubt as to their authentic value. She feels compelled to turn to God and say, " 'Why Lord, do you desire my works?' He answered: 'in order to see your will, daughter' " (Testimonies, 47). She now repeats: "Miserable are my services, even though I may have rendered many to my God. Why, then, must I remain in this miserable wretchedness? That the will of the Lord may be done."
These long-enduring sentiments, so rooted in her soul and still not eradicated, now find a prominent place in her prayer. She wants to shout out once more before God that life lasts too long. Particularly long is the feeling of waiting in uncertainty.
She wants to express to Him this interior liturgy of hers, concentrated in an offering of her desires. She would like the depths of this prayer of hers to take its effect on her works, to fill them with love. She tells herself, "Behold, the more you struggle the more you show the love you have for your God."
Teresa then opens her prayer to her readers: "May we all merit to love You, Lord, now that we must live, may we live for You."
Once again, the soliloquy recalls the words and sentiments of Saint Paul: "If we live, we live for Him. . . . Whether it be in life or in death, we belong to the Lord." What is important is "to please You" (1 Th 4:1). "O my Happiness and my God, what shall I do to please You?" And like Saint Paul who addressed himself to Christ: "What is it I must do, sir?" (Acts 22:10).

1. Woe is me, woe is me, Lord, how very long is this exile! And it passes with great sufferings of longing for my God! Lord, what can a soul placed in this prison do? O Jesus, how long is the life of man, even though it is said to be short! It is short, my God, for gaining through it a life that cannot end; but it is very long for the soul that desires to come into the presence of its God. What remedy do You provide for this suffering? There isn't any, except when one suffers for You.

2. O gentle Repose of my God's lovers! You don't fail anyone who loves You, since through You the torment the Beloved causes the soul desiring Him must both increase and be mitigated. I desire, Lord, to please You; but my happiness I know well doesn't lie with any mortal beings. Since this is true, You will not blame my desire. See me here, Lord; if it's necessary to live in order to render You some service, I

don't refuse all the trials that can come to me on earth, as Your lover
St. Martin said.

3. But alas, woe is me, Lord, for he had works and I have only
words, because I'm not good for anything else! May my desires be
worthwhile, my God, before Your divine Presence, and don't look at
my lack of merit. May we all merit to love You, Lord. Now that we
must live may we live for You, may our desires and self-interests come
to an end. What greater thing can be gained than to please You? O
my Happiness and my God, what shall I do to please You? Miserable
are my services, even though I may have rendered many to my God.
Why, then, must I remain in this miserable wretchedness? That the
will of the Lord may be done. What greater gain, my soul? Wait, wait,
for you know neither the day nor the hour. Watch with care, for
everything passes quickly, even though your desire make the certain
doubtful and the short time long. Behold the more you struggle the
more you show the love you have for your God and the more you will
rejoice in your Beloved with a joy and delight that cannot end.

107.
SIXTEENTH SOLILOQUY
YOU WOUNDED MY HEART

This present soliloquy is characterized by an ardent mystical prayer. Like certain prayerful persons in the Bible or in the history of the Church, Teresa feels wounded. She lives the "vehemence of love." She knows that "the heart that greatly loves" (Lk 7:42-46) accepts no reasoning.

This following soliloquy mirrors the outline of the Song of Songs: You wounded me (n. 1); I need you (n. 2); I will go out into the streets and squares crying out in search of you (n. 3). A poem of Saint John of the Cross is similar in form: "Where have you gone in hiding? Like a deer You fled. I followed after you crying out for you."

Teresa's prayer flows out from these three biblical themes. The first refers to an interior wound: you wounded my heart. This wound has been inflicted by a two-edged sword: his incomprehensible presence, while at the same time a state of loneliness. "The loneliness of being separated from God," while knowing and feeling that he is there, present "in all things." A wound of solitude and of absence that only he with his presence can alleviate.

She asks him out of the darkness of her faith: that he clearly manifest himself from amidst the obscurity that surrounds her. She asks this of him out of love: "O true Lover," heal me by means of your mercy, your sweetness, your joy, your comfort and through the "extraordinary signs of your love."

The second part develops the theme: I need you. "My lover belongs to me and I to him." The tide of love begins and ends in him. However, a response of love awakens with a prayer that "is not so lowly in rising from the creature to its Creator" (as has happened already to Augustine). Then follows the "war of love." During this period the verses her soul sang were very rousing:

> *"If the love, Lord, that you give to me*
> *is equal to the love I have for you,*
> *why do I feel this hesitancy,*
> *why are you holding back?"*

The third theme: to cry out in search. "I went in search crying out after you." Or as in the Song of Songs: to go out "to the squares and to the outskirts of the city having the daughters of Jerusalem promise that they would give her news about her God." In this moment it is not a matter of crying out a message to them or of relating her own experience. On the contrary, she needs them to tell her of her God. She needs him, who is present in all things, and who can arrive to us in all

ways. She hopes to find him, to abandon herself to him, to embrace him, and to remain united with him consumed in one fire: "Who can separate two burning blazes as these?" So, the soliloquy ends not so much in asking for his presence and union with him, but rather in the very experience of them. "At this point the two flames have become one single whirl of flames."
The reader is not required to keep a respectful distance from Teresa's experience. This prayer is an open invitation to allow oneself to be engulfed by this flame.

1. O true God and my Lord! It is a great consolation for the soul wearied by the loneliness of being separated from You to see that You are everywhere. But when the vehemence of love and the great impulses of this pain increase, there's no remedy, my God. For the intellect is disturbed and the reason is so kept from knowing the truth of Your omnipresence that it can neither understand nor know. It only knows it is separated from You and it accepts no remedy. For the heart that greatly loves receives no counsel or consolation except from the very one who wounded it, because from him it hopes its pain will be cured. When You desire, Lord, You quickly heal the wound You have caused; prior to this there is no hope for healing or joy, except for the joy of such worthwhile suffering.

2. O true Lover, with how much compassion, with how much gentleness, with how much delight, with how much favor and with what extraordinary signs of love You cure these wounds, which with the darts of this same love You have caused! O my God and my rest from all pains, how entranced I am! How could there be human means to cure what the divine fire has made sick? Who is there who knows how deep this wound goes, or how it came about, or how so painful and delightful a torment can be mitigated? It would be unreasonable were so precious a sickness able to be mitigated by something so lowly as are the means mortals can use. How right the bride of the Canticles is in saying: My Beloved is for me and I for my Beloved, for it is impossible that a love like this begin with something so lowly as is my love.

3. Well, if it is lowly, my Spouse, how is it that it is not so lowly in rising from the creature to its Creator? Oh, my God, why "I for my Beloved"? You, my true Lover, have begun this war of love, because this love doesn't seem to be anything else than a restlessness and dereliction on the part of all the faculties and senses; for they go out into the streets and squares entreating the daughters of Jerusalem to tell of their God. Once, Lord, this battle has begun, who are these faculties to fight against, if not against the one who has been made lord of this fortress where they dwell, which is the highest part of the

soul? They are driven out so that they might return to conquer their Conqueror. And now, tired of seeing themselves without Him, they quickly surrender and lose all their forces, and fight better; and by surrendering they win the victory over their Victor.

4. O my soul, what a wonderful battle you have waged in this pain, and how literally true is what happens here! Since my Beloved is for me and I for my Beloved, who will be able to separate and extinguish two fires so enkindled? It would amount to laboring in vain, for the two fires have become one.

108.
SEVENTEENTH SOLILOQUY
HAVE ME SERVE YOU ALWAYS
AND DO WHAT YOU DESIRE

"Desire from me what you want to desire; because this is what I want."
"May this 'I' die, and may another live in me greater than I and better for me than I."

This is the prayer of a contemplative immersed in the present, yet fixed in the presence of God. She is struck by waves of contrasting sentiments. To love, or let herself be loved. To desire, or to desire not. To will something on her own account, or to abandon herself to his will. To petition him once again for favors, or to beg him not to punish her by satisfying her desires. "Don't punish me by giving me what I want or desire if Your love, which lives in me always, doesn't desire it."
The soliloquy opens in a contemplative attitude: "O my God and my infinite Wisdom." "O Love that loves me more than I myself can love or understand." Seen from this sphere of love and infinite wisdom, all my wants and desires, my initiatives and words, including those I address to you in prayer, and with which I try to make known to you my requests, all become small and appear ambiguous and superfluous. Without leaving this contemplative sphere, Teresa presents to him a series of fleeting desires and projects: to work for him, to suffer for him, to serve him, to experience her misery, weakness and faintheartedness, "to fight against the storms of this world." To love and to attend to life and freedom.
Yet even all this seems small and limited. Services are uncertain. Freedom is "miserable captivity." Love is insufficient. Life is at "enmity with my true good," since there is always a risk to become ungrateful and a traitor. Teresa's prayer then turns back to its original contemplation: "May this 'I' die, and may another live in me." That my love may become "strong as death," and that I may see myself "thrown into this divine fire." That my free will may remain "fastened by the love of your Creator."
She is seized by such a strong desire to become "naturalized by the life of God," to enter into her repose, to "be drowned in the infinite sea of supreme truth," and to know what he knows, loving what he loves, enjoying what he enjoys. "He is blessed." "Blessed are those who are written in the book of this life."
The final words become lost in an uttering of psalmic themes, pronounced by the soul to itself. She concludes with a word addressed to God: "Don't abandon me, Lord, because I hope in You."

1. O my God and my infinite Wisdom, measureless and boundless and beyond all the human and the angelic intellects! O love that loves me more than I can love myself or understand! Why, Lord, do I want to desire more than what You want to give me? Why do I want to tire myself in asking You for something decreed by my desire? For with regard to everything my intellect can devise and my desire can want You've already understood my soul's limits, and I don't understand how my desire will help me. In this that my soul thinks it will gain, it will perhaps lose. For if I ask You to free me from a trial, and the purpose of that trial is my mortification, what is it that I'm asking for, my God? If I beg You to give the trial, it perhaps is not a suitable one for my patience, which is still weak and cannot suffer such a forceful blow. And if I suffer it with patience and am not strong in humility, it may be that I will think I've done something, whereas You do it all, my God. If I want to suffer, but not in matters in which it might seem unfitting for Your service that I lose my reputation – since as for myself I don't know of any concern in me about honor – it may be that for the very reason I think my reputation might be lost, more will be gained on account of what I'm seeking, which is to serve You.

2. I could say many more things about this, Lord, in order to explain that I don't understand myself. But since I know You understand these things, why am I speaking? So that when I awaken to my misery, my God, and see my blind reason, I might be able to see whether I find this misery in what I write. How often I see myself, my God, so wretched, weak, and fainthearted. For I go about looking for what your servant has done, since it already seemed to her she had received favors from You to fight against the tempests of this world. But no, my God, no; no more trust in anything I can desire for myself. Desire from me what You want to desire, because this is what I want; for all my good is in pleasing You. And if You, my God, should desire to please me by fulfilling all that my desire seeks, I see that I would be lost.

3. How miserable is the wisdom of mortals and uncertain their providence! May You through Your providence, Lord, provide the necessary means by which my soul may serve You at Your pleasure rather than at its own. Don't punish me by giving me what I want or desire if Your love, which lives in me always, doesn't desire it. May this "I" die, and may another live in me greater than I and better for me than I, so that I may serve Him. May He live and give me life. May He reign, and may I be captive, for my soul doesn't want any other liberty. How will he be free who is a stranger to the Most High? What greater or more miserable captivity than for a soul to be loosed from the hand of its Creator? Happy are those who with the strong fetter and chains of the kindness of the mercy of God find themselves

prisoners and deprived of the power to break loose. Love is strong as death, and unyielding as hell. Oh, that I might be slain by Him and thrown into this divine hell where there is no longer any hope of coming out; or better, any fear of finding oneself outside! But, woe is me, Lord; while this mortal life lasts, eternal life is ever in danger!

4. O life at enmity with my good; who has leave to bring you to an end? I bear with you because God bears with you; I maintain you because you are His; do not be a traitor or ungrateful to me.

Nonetheless, woe is me, Lord, for my exile is long! Short is all life in exchange for Your eternity; very long is one day alone and one hour for whoever doesn't know and who fears whether he will offend You! O free will, so much the slave of your freedom if you don't live fastened with fear and love of your Creator! Oh, when will that happy day arrive when you will see yourself drowned in the infinite sea of supreme truth, where you will no longer be free to sin! Nor will you want to sin, for you will be safe from every misery, naturalized by the life of your God!

5. He is blessed, because He knows, loves, and rejoices in Himself without any other thing being possible. He neither has nor can have—nor would He be a perfect God if He did have—the freedom to forget Himself or cease loving Himself. Then, my soul, you will enter into your rest when you become intimate with this supreme Good, understand what He understands, love what He loves, and rejoice in what gives Him joy. Now, you will find you've lost your changeable will; now, there shall be no more change! For God's grace will have done so much that by it you will be so perfect a sharer in His divine nature that you shall no longer be able, or want to be able, to forget the supreme Good or fail to enjoy Him together with His love.

6. Blessed are those who are written in the book of this life. But you, my soul, if you are written there, why are you sad and why do you disturb me? Hope in God, for even now I will confess to Him my sins and His mercies. And putting these all together, I shall make a song of praise with perpetual sights to my Savior and my God. There may come a day when my glory will sing to Him, and when my conscience will not feel compunction, where all sighs and fears will have ceased; but in the meantime, in silence and hope will be my strength. I want to live and die in striving and hoping for eternal life more than for the possession of all creatures and all their goods; for these will come to an end. Don't abandon me, Lord, because I hope that in You my hope will not be confounded; may I always serve You; and do with me whatever You will.

BLESSINGS AND SHORT SONGS OF PRAISE

*In one of her interior monologues, Teresa, as a psalmist, tells herself: "Oh, my soul, bless forever so great a God" (*Soliloquy, 3:2).

Blessing God is a form of biblical prayer: Zechariah blesses the Lord God of Israel, the angel blesses Mary, on Palm Sunday the people sing praises to Jesus, the prophets, the three youth in the furnace, and psalmists interweave an immense symphony of blessings.

It is normal that a spontaneous and original form of blessing emerge from the soul of a prayerful Christian like Francis of Assisi, Catherine of Siena, or the Curé of Ars.

The same holds true for what flows from the soul and pen of Teresa of Jesus. Her phrases "may He be blessed" can go on without end.

To bless God, Christ, His Majesty ("may He be blessed" she will say in deepest respect). The motives for these blessings are numerous and stem from any kind of pretext.

*Because He is who He is, because His reign is without end, because his mercy is baffling, for all He has forgiven Teresa, for that which He has suffered and hoped for, for the graces He has given her. For the Virgin Mary, for the Church and the Eucharist, for the sake of others, for the poor, for scholars, for benefactors, for enemies. Teresa blesses Him above all for her own story of salvation. Without being a priest, Teresa enjoys what she calls "sending blessings." To a friend in Toledo she writes, "I think of you at times, and have sent blessings to you" (*Letter, 420:3). *To her great friend Gracian: "How many blessings this old daughter of yours has sent you" (*Letter, 99:1). *Or to her Sisters at Seville: "Many blessings have I sent to you. The blessings of Our Lady and of the Most Holy Trinity" (*Letter, 242:16).

Therefore, we can say that these phrases "may He be blessed" which are directed toward God appear throughout the pages of this saint's writings. They emerge as she calls to mind a vehement transport of the past. At times, they mark the conclusion of an emotional account, or the epilogue of a simple episode, yet lived with a sense of salvation history. They become even more pronounced when she recalls certain mystical graces.

So, in scattering these blessings throughout her writings, she reveals her prayer that was a fruit of life. To read them is to pray and to feel moved to pronounce the same words of praise and blessings from the depths of one's own life.

Each of the following blessings is preceded by a simple note that describes their setting.

Oh, my soul,
bless forever so great a God!
(*Soliloquy*, 3:2)

109.

Simply recalling the words of the Creed: "Your reign will have no end," gives her "particular joy."

I praise You, O Lord, and I bless You and may all things praise You, for Your kingdom will last forever.

(*Way*, E 37:1)

110.

Bearing in mind the story of her own calling, she blesses God saying:

Oh, God help me! What means His Majesty was employing to prepare me for the state in which He desired to make use of me! For without my desiring it, He forced me to overcome my repugnance. May He be blessed forever. Amen.

(*Life*, 3:4)

111.

During her very first attempts to prepare herself for prayer:

May He be blessed by all, for I have seen clearly that He does not fail to repay, even in this life, every good desire.

(*Life*, 4:10)

May You be blessed, Lord, who put up with me so long!

(*Life*, 2:8)

112.

In recalling the terrible sickness which struck her during her youth, her breakdown, and the four days spent in a coma, she blesses God:

May He be blessed forever. May it please His Majesty that I die rather than ever cease to love Him.

(*Life*, 5:11)

113.

Everything in her life has changed. She now lives immersed in the experience of God. She blesses him in the same tone:

When I see what patience God has had with me and see myself in this state, it doesn't take much to lose the thread of what I'm saying and intend to say. May it please the Lord that my follies be always like these, and may His Majesty no longer allow me to have the power to offend Him the least bit; rather, may I be consumed in this prayer.

(Life, 19:9)

114.

Calling to mind her times of unfaithfulness:

May You be blessed forever! Although I abandoned You, You did not abandon me.

(Life, 6:9)

115.

After recalling her years of struggle and mediocrity:

And I praise the mercy of God, for it was He alone who gave me His hand. May He be blessed forever and ever. Amen.

(Life, 7:22)

116.

She tells of her conversion and then exclaims:

May God be praised who gave me the life to rise up from a death so deadly.

(Life, 9:8)

117.

As she speaks of the garden of her soul and of the levels of prayer:

May God be blessed for everything, who desires and consents that someone like myself should speak about His graces, so lofty and so sublime.

(Life, 12:7)

118.

After recalling and praising the knowledge of scholars, who are light for her and for others, she says:

May You be blessed, Lord, who have made me so unable and unprofitable! But I praise You very much because You awaken so many to awaken us.

(Life, 13:21)

May You be blessed forever, Lord! May all things praise You forever!

(Life, 16:4)

119.

For the mystical graces she has received, in particular for union with God and the experience of his divine presence within her:

O my Lord, how good You are! May You be blessed forever! May all things praise You, my God, for You have so loved us that we can truthfully speak of this communication which You engage in with souls even in our exile! And even in the case of those who are good, this still shows great generosity and magnanimity. In fact, it is Your communication, my Lord; and You give it in the manner of who You are. O infinite Largess, how magnificent are Your works!

(Life, 18:3)

120.

On a particular page, rich in its content and advice, Teresa states: "It [the soul] should trust in the goodness of God, which is greater than all the evils we are capable of. And He doesn't remember our ingratitude when we, although knowing about it, desire to return to His friendship; nor does He remember the favors He bestowed on us that could become further reason for his punishing us. Such favors, on the contrary, help us to receive pardon more quickly as members of His household who have eaten, as I say, from His table. Souls should remember His words and see what He did with me; I became tired of offending Him, yet all the while He never tired of forgiving me. He never tires of giving, nor can He exhaust His mercies. Let us not tire of receiving."

May He be blessed forever, amen — and may all things praise Him.

(Life, 19:15)

Blessed be the Lord who is so good. Amen.

(Life, 20:16)

You do so much in coming to a dwelling place as shabby as mine. May You be blessed forever and ever!

(Life, 22:17)

121.

Teresa recalls a very particular grace: her definitive healing from sentimental attachments. She concludes her account with these words:

May God be blessed forever because in an instant He gave me the freedom that I with all the efforts of many years could not attain by myself, often trying so to force myself that my health had to pay dearly.

(Life, 24:8)

Blessed be the Lord who has so truly helped me!

(Life, 25:22)

122.

A decree of the Inquisition leaves Teresa without any books to read. This is painful for her, but an inner voice tells her: "I will give you a living book."

His Majesty had become the true book in which I saw the truths. Blessed be such a book that leaves what must be read and done so impressed that you cannot forget!

(Life, 26:5)

123.

Teresa, when recalling her first Christological experiences, is marvelled at the Lord's beauty and glory:

May He be blessed forever! So much glory would have been unbearable next to so lowly and wretched a subject as I; and as one who knew this, the merciful Lord was preparing me.

(Life, 28:1)

124.

At the conclusion of the chapter in which she speaks of her strong impulses of love and of the grace of her intellectual visions:

May He be blessed forever who grants so many favors to one who responds so poorly to gifts as great as these.

(Life, 29:14)

125.

Teresa concludes chapter 30 in this way: "For such a soul doesn't know or understand the blessing it has unless it has experienced a taste of what it is to be unable to do anything in the service of the Lord."

May He be blessed for everything, and may the angels give Him glory, amen.

(Life, 30:21)

126.

After referring to a vision of hell which she received:

May You be blessed, my God, forever! How obvious it is that You loved me much more than I did myself!

(Life, 32:5)

127.

After giving an account of the difficulties involved in the founding of her first Carmel:

May He be blessed who in this way did everything, amen.

(Life, 33:16)

128.

Drawing a final balance on the graces she received, simply calling them to mind moves her to say, "I don't know how one could live":

May He be blessed and praised forever and ever! May it please His Majesty, by the blood His Son shed for me, since He has desired that I understand something of so many great blessings and in some way begin to enjoy them, that what happened to Lucifer, who through his

own fault lost everything, may not happen to me. May He because of
who He is not allow it.

(*Life,* 38:7)

May He be blessed forever who gives so much, and to whom I give
so little.

(*Life,* 39:6)

May He be blessed who when He so desires draws good out of
everything, amen.

(*Life,* 39:14)

129.

Concluding The Book of Her Life, *and before drawing a balance on
the graces she received:* "Many times I have been frightened over this
vision of what I have written. . . . How can I go on living after seeing
these things and then looking at myself":

May He be blessed forever who has put up with so much from me!

(*Life,* 40:11)

May He be blessed forever who has taken such care of me.

(*Life,* 40:17)

130.

When beginning a lesson on poverty and the spirit of detachment:

May You be blessed forever, my God, and may all creatures praise
You . . . for my vocation to be a nun was a very great favor!

(*Way,* 8:2)

131.

*In commenting on the sentence "Forgive us, Lord, as we forgive
others":*

Help me, O God, for the world has turned upside down. Blessed be
the Lord who has taken us from its grasp.

(*Way,* E 63:3)

May His name be blessed forever. Amen. I beg the Eternal Father
to forgive my debts and my great sins. Though I have never had cause

to have to forgive others on their account, I myself have much each day to be forgiven. And may He grant me the grace to be in the position one day to have something to offer as a backing for something to request.

(*Way,* E 65:3)

132.

The final words of The Way of Perfection

May the Lord be blessed and praised; from Him comes every good we speak of, think about, and do. Amen.

(*Way,* 42:7)

133.

The following verses are taken from her Interior Castle. *At the end of the first page of her book she writes:*

I always am, and will be, and have been subject to her [the Church]. May He be always blessed and glorified, amen.

(*Castle,* Prologue, 3)

134.

The fifth dwelling places. In front of the mystery of a God who lowers himself to the point of establishing "union" with mankind who loves him:

Blessed be His mercy that wants so much to be humbled!

(*Castle,* V, 4:3)

Oh, great delight, to suffer in doing the will of God!

(*Castle,* V, 2:14)

May it please His Majesty that we may merit to render Him some service; without as many faults as we always have, even in good works, amen.

(*Castle,* V, 4:11)

135.

The sixth dwelling places. The conclusion of a chapter in which she tells of lofty mystical graces:

May it please His Majesty to give us the courage so that we may merit to serve Him, amen.

(Castle, VI, 5:12)

136.

In front of the humanity of Christ. Love and a profession of faith in meditating on his holy humanity:

I wouldn't want any good save that acquired through Him from whom all blessings come to us. May He be always praised, amen.

(Castle, VI, 7:15)

May the divine Majesty provide a remedy that will enable us to place our eyes only on pleasing Him and to be forgetful of ourselves, as I said, amen.

(Castle, VI, 3:18)

137.

The seventh dwelling places. The conclusion of the chapter in which she spoke about the state of the soul that has arrived at the culmination of sanctity:

May He be ever blessed and praised by all His creatures, amen.

(Castle, VII, 3:15)

138.

Prior to treating the topic of the trinitarian indwelling, which she is hesitant to do, she writes:

May God be praised and understood a little more, and let all the world cry out against me; how much more so in that I will perhaps be dead when what I write is seen. May He be blessed who lives, and will live, forever, amen.

(Castle, VII, 1:2)

139.

The conclusion of The Interior Castle. *Teresa renews her act of submission to the Church: "And I submit in everything to what the holy Roman Catholic Church holds, for in this Church I live, declare my faith, and promise to live and die" (*Castle, *Epilogue, 4).*

May it please His Majesty, my Sisters and daughters, that we all reach that place where we may ever praise Him. Through the merits of His Son who lives and reigns forever and ever, may He give me the grace to carry out something of what I tell you, amen.

May God our Lord be forever praised and blessed, amen.

(Castle, VII, 4:16 and Epilogue, 4)

140.

In considering the verse of the Songs of Songs: "Let him kiss me with kisses of his mouth!" she writes:

O my Lord and my God, and what words are these that a worm speaks them to its Creator! May You be blessed, Lord, for in so many ways have You taught us! But who will dare, my King, utter these words without Your permission?

(Meditations, 1:10)

141.

Calling to mind the graces which the Lord showered upon the first novices of the Teresian Carmels:

May He be ever blessed, amen. In order to love, it doesn't seem that He waits for anything else than to be loved.

(Foundations, 3:18)

All must come from His hand. May He be blessed forever.

(Foundations, 5:17)

142.

After giving an account of the moving story of a great benefactor of the Carmel of Valladolid, Bernardino de Mendoza:

May He be blessed and praised for everything. For He repays our lowly deeds with eternal life and glory, and He makes them great while they are in fact of little value.

(Foundations, 10:5)

143.

Teresa concludes her report on the foundation of the Carmel of Segovia:

May His name be ever blessed who has always granted me so many
favors, and may all creatures praise Him. Amen.

(Foundations, 21:11)

144.

*At the end of her account on the foundation of the Carmel of
Caravaca:*

May He who has done everything be blessed and may charity be
awakened in the persons who have helped us. May it please His Majesty
to protect us always and give us His grace so that we will not be
ungrateful for so many favors, amen.

(Foundations, 27:16)

145.

*She describes the background of a sad and difficult undertaking. An
accumulation of all kinds of circumstances. Years marked by the
prohibition of founding Carmels: "I felt that I was the cause of all
this torment and that if I, like Jonah, were to be thrown into the sea,
this storm would pass." False accusations were also made against Saint
Teresa. She writes:*

May God who favors truth be praised! . . . May it please His Majesty
that this all be for His honor and glory.

(Foundations, 28:6)

May You be blessed, my Lord and my God, for You are unchange-
able forever and ever, amen. The one who serves unto the end will live
without end in Your eternity.

(Foundations, 27:21)

146.

*The acquisition of a house for the Carmel of Palencia proved very
successful:*

May He who enlightened me in this regard be blessed forever and
ever. . . . It seems our Lord desires me and all others to know that it
is only His Majesty who does these works. . . . Blessed be His mercy,
amen.

(Foundations, 29:24)

147.

After giving a description of the foundation of the Carmel of Soria:

May He be blessed and praised from age to age, amen. Thanks be to God.

(Foundations, 30:14)

148.

Her last account of the Foundations: *the one of Burgos which was a very wearisome task. Finally, Teresa and her Sisters opened the cloister, and for this she blesses God:*

Oh, my Spouse, true God and true man! Should this favor be taken so lightly? Let us praise Him, my Sisters, because He has granted it to us and let us not tire of praising so great a King and Lord, who has prepared for us a kingdom without end in exchange for some little troubles which will end tomorrow and which come wrapped in a thousand joys. May He be blessed forever, amen, amen.

(Foundations, 31:47)

149.

The last words of The Book of Her Foundations:

Blessed be the Lord who so carefully looks after the affairs of His servants! May He be blessed forever, amen.

(Foundations, Epilogue, 5)

150.

An ingenuous hymn of thanksgiving, after telling of the special grace of God which entrusts her with the mission of being a foundress and a wanderer:

O greatness of God! How You manifest Your power in giving courage to an ant! How true, my Lord, that it is not because of You that those who love You fail to do great works but because of our own cowardice and pusillanimity. Since we are never determined, but full of human prudence and a thousand fears, You, consequently, my God, do not do your marvelous and great works. Who is more fond than You of giving, or of serving even at a cost to Yourself, when there is someone open to receive it? May it please Your Majesty that

I render You some service and that I not have to render an accounting
for all that I have received, amen.

(Foundations, 2:7)

PRAYER AND POETRY

For both Saint Teresa and Saint John of the Cross, poetry is the soul's celebration. They introduced into the first Carmels the poetic rite, the religious sense of beauty and the recourse to poetry to underline personal and communitarian joy.

Mother Teresa — who in her own opinion was not a poet — abandoned herself to inspiration and composed verses especially for two particular circumstances: for communal celebration like the arrival of Christmas or the Profession of one of the Sisters (at Carmel, Profession is a wedding ceremony); or to celebrate her own inner joy at having received great mystical graces.

For the former, she would compose verses that could be placed into song. For the latter, her lyrical impulses would readily induce her to prayer.

We have gathered here just a few of her verses, selected from the best of her poems. They are deeply religious in meaning and at times their crystalline transparency reveals the mystical character of her experience that inspired them.

151.

A contemplation of the beauty of Christ. Teresa, like Saint Paul, has seen the Risen Lord. She saw his glory and his beauty: "The vision of Christ left upon me an impression of His most extraordinary beauty." "Upon beholding Your person one sees immediately that You alone, on account of the majesty You reveal, merit to be called Lord" (Life, 37:4, 6). Saint Paul exclaimed: "O height, depth, and breadth." Saint Teresa: "O beauty . . ."

Oh Beauty exceeding
All other beauties!
Paining, but You wound not
Free of pain You destroy
The love of creatures

Oh, knot that binds
Two so different,
Why do You become unbound
For when held fast You strengthen
Making injuries seem good.

Bind the one without being
With being unending;
Finish, without finishing,
Love, without having to love,
Magnify our nothingness.

152.

One of Saint Teresa's poems is entitled: "About those words 'My lover belongs to me.'" Like all the great mystics, Teresa was very struck by the words of the Song of Songs: "My lover belongs to me and I to him." These words reveal the highest experience of love and the synthesis of that union which is the apex toward which Christian prayer definitively tends. This is the first stanza.

Myself surrendered and given,
The exchange is this:
My Beloved is for me,
And I am for my Beloved.

153.

*A prayer and a madrigal (lyrical poem) of love. Saint Teresa, more than just once, addressed herself to Christ or to God under the renowned "pretence" of Saint John of the Cross: the need "to love God as much as you are loved by Him" (*The Spiritual Canticle, *38:4). With this same boldness of love, Teresa composes the "loving conversation" that begins in this way:*

If the love You have for me
Is like the love I have for You,
My God, what detains me?
Oh, what is delaying You?

154.

The prayer of one who has undergone a conversion. Teresa feels to be in fine tune with the biblical figure of Saint Paul, who in the moment of his conversion meets Christ and holds a brief dialogue with Him: "Lord, what do You want of me?" It is the Apostle's first Christian prayer. Teresa makes this prayer her own and comments on it.

Majestic Sovereign,
Unending wisdom,
Kindness pleasing to my soul;
God sublime, one Being Good,
Behold this one so vile.
Singing of her love to you:
What do You want of me?

Yours, you made me,
Yours, you saved me,
Yours, you endured me,
Yours, you called me,
Yours, you awaited me,
Yours, I did not stray.
What do You want of me?

Give me death, give me life,
Health or sickness,
Honor or shame,
War or swelling peace,
Weakness or full strength,
Yes, to these I say,
What do You want of me?

155.

"I die because I do not die" is the refrain to some of Teresa's verses, which recall the rhythm of certain secular songs. However, the prayer contained within blossoms forth from a deep Christological experience, from the desire for a definitive meeting with Christ. Once again we sense an echo to the sentiments and expressions of Saint Paul: "and the life I live now is not my own; Christ is living in me," which in Teresa becomes: "I live outside of myself. . . . I die of love. . . . I live now in the Lord who has desired me for Himself."

> *I live without living in myself,*
> Since I die of love,
> Living apart from love,
> I live now in the Lord,
> Who has desired me for Himself.
> He inscribed on my heart
> When I gave it to Him:
> *I die because I do not die.*
>
> Within this divine prison,
> Of love in which I live,
> My God my captive is.
> My heart is free
> To behold my prisoner-God,
> Passion welling in my heart,
> *I die because I do not die.*
>
> That life from above,
> That is true life,
> Until this life dies,
> Life is not enjoyed.
> Death, be not aloof;
> In dying first, may life be,
> *I die because I do not die.*

156.

A psalm of desires. Teresa, more than with the biblical psalmist, feels in tune with the experience of Saint Paul, full of the desire to die so as to be with Christ (cf. Phil 1:23). She repeats it in the refrain to each of the stanzas: "Longing to see You, death I desire."

> My God, how sad is
> Life without You!

Longing to see You,
Death I desire.

Master, my soul
In vain seeks You!
Always unseen
You leave me anxiously longing.
Ah! the very longing inflames
Until I cry out:
Longing to see You,
Death I desire.

When at last
You enter my heart,
My God, then at once
I fear your leaving.
The pain that touches me
Makes me say,
Longing to see You,
Death I desire.

157.

In front of the cross of Jesus Christ. On September 14, the Feast of the Exultation of the Cross, a penitential lenten period begins in the Teresian communities. It is a feastday for the community. In this context, Teresa's cry expressed in the refrain: "O Cross, my welcome be," acquires its true meaning.

O Cross, my life's delightful rest
My welcome be.

Beneath your protecting banner
Even the weakest are made strong
O life of our death,
Reviving it so well.
Having tamed the lion,
By you he was slain:
My welcome be.

158.

An interior monologue in the mode of the psalms of wisdom. Teresa examines her personal convictions. She descends their order of value

*until she reaches the bottom. She makes her profession of faith: the
typical creed of a contemplative: "God alone suffices."*

Let nothing trouble you,
Let nothing scare you,
All is fleeting,
God alone is unchanging.
Patience
Everything obtains.
Who possesses God
Nothing wants.
God alone suffices.

159.

*Poetry and communitarian prayer. There is festivity in the home: the
perpetual profession of one of the young Sisters of the community.
Mother Teresa celebrates the occasion with some of her verses that
reflect this particular circumstance. In the first poem, she cries out for
a militant spirit; in the second, her words are an idyll (poetic
description) of matrimony.*

*All who serve in the army
Beneath this banner,
Sleep no longer, sleep no more,
For now there is no earthly peace.*

Not one coward will there be!
Let us risk our lives!
None better guards it
Than he who loses it!
Our guide is Jesus,
The reward of this warring.
*Sleep no longer, sleep no more.
For there is no peace on earth.*

*

*Oh, what good unequalled!
Oh, marriage most sacred!
That the King of Majesty,
Should be Betrothed.*

Ah, wondrous happening

Ready now for you!
God wants His bride
Having won you by His death!
In serving Him be strong
For you are vowed to this.
Already the King of Majesty
Is your Betrothed.

EPILOGUE

160.
"LET US PRAY" . . . IN PRIVATE

Teresa writes a letter to her brother Lawrence, who has just returned from the Americas, and has already been practicing mystical prayer through his sister's teaching (cf. Letter of January 17, 1577). She had told him in private of the immense graces she had received during the past Christmas: "How good the Lord is . . . My raptures have returned . . . I am almost like an inebriated woman these days. In this way, at least I realize that my soul is in a good position." She concludes by inviting him to associate himself to her with this form of a "let us pray."

It is good that we praise our Lord one for another; you, at least, do it for me, because I am incapable of thanking Him as I should, and consequently need much help to do so.

161.
HER LAST PRAYERS

Saint Teresa did not write down her last prayers. They were handed down to us, in fragmented form, through her nurse Sister Anna of Saint Bartholomew and her niece Teresita, a novice at the Carmel of Alba de Tormes.
"She asked them to bring her Holy Communion, because she felt as though she were dying. When she saw that they were approaching, she rose up in her bed with such energy that she had to be restrained. It seemed as though she wanted to hurl herself out of bed. With great joy she said:

My Lord, it is time to move on. Well then, may Your will be done!

This eyewitness (Teresita) saw her and heard her thank God many times over, even with a strong voice, because he had made her a daughter of the Church and she hoped to be saved as a member of the Church, through the Passion and the Blood of Christ our Lord.

She then began to pronounce words that were very tender and full of love:

O my Lord and my Spouse, the hour that I have so desired has come. It's time for us to meet one another."

Also available from New City Press:

IN SEARCH OF GOD

by W. Herbstrith (with Teresa of Avila, John of the Cross, Therese of Lisieux, Edith Stein)

"Herbstrith's message is not that mysticism is easy, but simply that the way of mysticism is open to everyone. . . . Her study of this quartet of Carmelite saints is a vital word on silent prayer and on a spirituality of belief."

"The theology is lucid and the biographies are simple, together opening up a beautiful mystical path through the forest of ordinary experience."

B.C. Catholic

"[The author] writes to 'present ideas that stem from a tradition of Christian meditation' shared by the four Carmelite heroes. An introduction to the four, this book might be helpful to those who want to begin to 'stress the fact that mystical life means to abandon oneself to the closeness of our living God.' "

National Catholic Reporter

"Waltraud Herbstrith, is a Carmelite, also known as Sr. Teresa a Matre Dei (OCD), from Cologne. There's some 'how to' for meditators here, plus short exegeses of passages and sayings by the above mentioned mentors."

The Christian Century

"This is a helpful primer on spiritual life. . . ."

Spectrum Review, Integral Publishing

"Enjoyable reading."

Kindred Spirits

Series "Spirituality"
ISBN 0-911728-69-9, paper, 128 pp.

MEDITATIONS

by Chiara Lubich

6th printing

"[A] collection of brief but intensely meaningful thoughts carefully mined from the scriptures. Like shafts of sunlight that break through the clouds on a dreary day, these meditations touch us and turn our most mundane activities into brightly lit God-moments. Chiara helps us to see all the events of our lives as opportunities for our ultimate . . . perfection."

Liguorian

"Chiara Lubich . . . is a leading figure in ecumenism and the dialogue between Christianity and other world religions. This is a collection of her meditations based on her experience of living the gospel."

Theology Digest

"Her experience, intuitions, and understanding . . . have inspired millions throughout the world."

Institute of Formative Spirituality

Series "Christian Living: A Spirituality of Unity"
ISBN 0-911782-20-6, paper, 134 pp.